RAISING a
THOUGHTFUL
TEENAGER

Also by Ben Kamin

STONES IN THE SOUL:
One Day in the Life of
an American Rabbi

RAISING a
THOUGHTFUL
TEENAGER

A Book of Answers
and Values for Parents

Rabbi Ben Kamin

A DUTTON BOOK

DUTTON

Published by the Penguin Group
Penguin Books USA Inc., 375 Hudson Street, New York,
New York 10014, U.S.A.
Penguin Books Ltd, 27 Wrights Lane, London W8 5TZ, England
Penguin Books Australia Ltd, Ringwood, Victoria, Australia
Penguin Books Canada Ltd, 10 Alcorn Avenue,
Toronto, Ontario, Canada M4V 3B2
Penguin Books (N.Z.) Ltd, 182–190 Wairau Road,
Auckland 10, New Zealand

Penguin Books Ltd, Registered Offices:
Harmondsworth, Middlesex, England

First published by Dutton, an imprint of Dutton Signet,
a division of Penguin Books USA Inc.
Distributed in Canada by McClelland & Stewart Inc.

First Printing, January, 1996
1 3 5 7 9 10 8 6 4 2

 REGISTERED TRADEMARK—MARCA REGISTRADA

LIBRARY OF CONGRESS CATALOGING-IN-PUBLICATION DATA
Kamin, Ben.
Raising a thoughtful teenager: a book of answers and values for parents
p.   cm.
ISBN 0–525–93984–9
1. Jewish teenagers—Conduct of life.   2. Parent and teenager—
Religious aspects—Judaism.   3. Pastoral counseling (Judaism)
4. Ethics, Jewish.   I. Title.
BM727.K36   1995
296.7'4—dc20   95–34937
                                                                CIP

Printed in the United States of America
Set in New Caladonia
Designed by Jesse Cohen

For my daughters, Sari and Debra,
two reasons for breathing

CONTENTS

ACKNOWLEDGMENTS

This book is a result of the work I do, every day, as a rabbi. My congregants at The Temple-Tifereth Israel in Cleveland continue to touch and inform my life. I have the privilege of seeing and hearing parents and children mingling their feelings, their joys, their anger during sometimes delicate moments. In this book I have often drawn upon experiences from within the congregational family. Fictitious names are usually used when relating an incident. However, I have infringed upon the private stories of real people and do not take this access for granted.

Susan Belman dedicated a great deal of time in reviewing and commenting on the manuscript. I am grateful for her insights. Much appreciation is also felt for the host of young people who shared their concerns with me as I developed the themes of this book.

I am proud to acknowledge the constant support and wisdom of my literary agent, Faith Hamlin. I am equally as fortunate to work with my editor at Dutton, Deb Brody—a real friend and a person of discriminating standards.

My family understands more than can be written in this space; my wife, Cathy, is the one who invented love.

INTRODUCTION

A lmost every book I pick up about teenagers and their parents begins with pretty much the same sentence: "It is not easy raising teenagers in this day and age." Well, that's true—on some days. On some days it is very easy, because there are days when our teenaged children are delightful, funny, warm, and lovable. On other days, they are stubborn, thorny, reclusive, or just plain incorrigible. On one day, you feel like physically shaking your kid out of her impossible disposition. The next day, you can't let go of her; you stroke her hair, you rub her face, and you thank goodness you were given the gift of such a child.

Many years of being around teenagers have convinced me that formulas do not necessarily work with them. When they have questions, a parent can consult with a psychology manual. But by the time the answer is formulated and converted into plain language, the youngster has already moved on to his or her boom box, to MTV, or back to the telephone. Teenagers in the 1990s move quickly, and they are used to getting information instantly. In some ways, they are no different than teenagers of any age: They have hormones, anxieties, and mood swings. But this group also has earphones, computer terminals, and cable converter boxes. When we do get their attention, I'm not so sure they want us to be therapists. They just want us to be parents.

Many books are written for teenagers by clinical professionals and these texts offer some insights in a complicated era. But kids are not theoretical—they are real. I have found over time that when they have questions about things, they react best and they focus most clearly on a response that is direct and distinct. They really do think a lot about what they see on television, what they hear in school, what they read in the newspaper. Sometimes they want to talk about it, sometimes they don't. Sometimes they are very tight-lipped, sometimes they just won't shut up. I like them a lot because, in this ongoing contradiction, they are truly human. I think, therefore, that we adults ought to be truly humane.

There are a number of books for parents and children that are written in a religious vein. I am a congregational rabbi, and I certainly draw from my tradition and its many insights about human life. The Jewish people have been trying to interpret this life from the times of the Bible through to the close of this difficult and frightening century. Nevertheless, I feel very strongly that teenagers live in the real world, and the issues that trouble or inspire them have to do with what they see and hear in day-to-day life. Theological answers are fine for heaven, but our kids live on the earth. Indeed, we want to keep them safe in *this* world. There are times when young people like to meditate, and many of their questions have to do with God and mortality and the meaning of their lives. Basically, however, when a youngster has a question, he's not looking for a prayer. He's looking for an answer.

In fact, we parents and professionals are accountable to young people—here and now. They live in a fast society of drive-through burgers and drive-by bullets. Our first responsibility to them is to preserve their childhood for as long as reasonably possible, in spite of a ferocious culture that wants their time, their money, and their innocence.

They look to us for nourishment and for protection. We don't always have the solutions to their problems, but we must at least try to have answers to their questions.

"Who am I?" and "Do I account for anything?" are two questions I see young people asking themselves with increasing and painful frequency. I often tell them that the word *me* has the numerical value of one, and that in the numeral one lies the unique power of every single human being. "You are the only *you* that there ever was or will ever be," I'll say, trying to encourage a young person's sense of distinctiveness.

This quality of "individuality" is marketed heavily on the talk shows and in the ubiquitous advice columns. Therapists, preachers, and a number of celebrities like to exhort kids to be self-validated, and to carry on with a healthy amount of personal esteem. That's fine, but parents must be individuals as well. While adults have been looking for the youngsters to emerge, they have been looking for us as well. I have rarely met a teenager who could not gain some-thing positive from a focused, truly mutual encounter with that sometimes elusive, carpool-managing, undoubtedly caring person who is, after all, that kid's mom or dad.

It's not that difficult to make contact with your teen-ager. All your child really needs is *you*. That son or daugh-ter of yours has got to feel, deep inside, that you are right there for him or her. A thousand social or electrical dis-tractions are waiting to sweep that youngster's need for you away from your family life. What could possibly justify any lack of attentiveness to your own child, who is coping with so much?

When he brings you his questions, all you have to do to succeed is to concentrate on him. When she is feeling uncertain, what she does not need is to be less than certain about your involvement in her life. More than the answers themselves, these kids need to feel that we truly acknowl-edge their questions. The method I have to offer in this book, along with the questions and answers I am present-ing, is what I call "the Three L's" of good parent-teen dynamics:

1. Look.
2. Listen.
3. Love.

When our teenaged youngsters come to us with their concerns, their anxieties, or even just their playfulness, we need to look right at them. They need to find our eyes upon them, and they need to feel wholly satisfied that we are truly engaged by the sight of them. Eye contact is crucial; if they think that we are not even looking, there is little hope for a dialogue. Look upon them—and their funny earrings, or their strangely dyed or beaded hair, or their painted fingernails, or their peculiar head wear—without being judgmental. It may be that what we regard as a bizarre fashion statement is actually designed to get us to look at them. And when we begin to look, and we notice the texture of their skin, the color of their eyes, the shape of their growing and unwieldy bodies, we may begin to remember that they are, after all, the flesh and blood we brought into the world. Look at them!

Next, you must listen, in order to be able to hear. It is perhaps hard to imagine just how many sources of noise come into your house, separating you from your child. From the power lines outside, resonating through cable wires, phone circuits, radio lines and so many other kinds of audio hardware and energy fibers, come countless sources of intense, diverting modulation. Further separating you from your own child's frequency are the personal earphones you and he are both given to wear in the house. Sooner or later, every individual in the home has achieved the very best sound, but nobody is listening to anybody else. The human heart has a graphic equalizer as well; it is never the wrong time for a parent to adjust it and really hear the words coming out of a child's mouth. Listen to them!

Finally, and most importantly, love the child who stands before you, delighting you, frustrating you, mesmerizing you, boring you. Even if you are angry at her, or if you are disappointed with her, love her. Our love for these children—these kinetic, hyperactive, overprogrammed, and bombarded children—must be absolutely unconditional. No children since the creation of the world have ever had to know more, integrate more, sift through more. And yet, under all the hype, beyond the music videos, past all the jive, are feeling, trembling kids with a great capacity for feeling lonely. We must discipline them, guide them, feed and clothe them. But most of all, we must love them.

It is my strong contention that no matter how difficult their questions, how inappropriate their behavior may be at a given moment, no matter how much they try us with their attitudes, their requests, and their demands, we must start with love. If you start and finish with love, no question—from sex to drugs to interfaith dating—will be concluded without some form of an answer. Love them! It was the Jewish biblical tradition that first offered the admonition to "love your neighbor as yourself." How much more so are we to openly love the child who lives in the same house as us, and who is the flesh and blood of ourselves.

My younger daughter, Debra, likes to say about herself, "Yeah, me!" When she does something well, or when she acknowledges the accolades of her friends, her teachers or her peers, she enjoys this short burst of self-congratulation and relief. I feel happy when I hear Debra indulge herself in this way, because I know that she is feeling positive about herself.

Indeed, we are born one by one, even in this era of mass assembly lines but, in spite of the current emphasis on self-esteem, I find it is still hard to teach a teenager the hallowed meaning of being oneself. Judaism teaches that each one of us has a separate quality that defines ourselves. Surely every caring parent wants his or her child to have such a clarifying separateness, which both distinguishes and safeguards our child from the world at large.

We parents and professionals would want youngsters to revere such a separateness, but today's world often works against our ability to make such a distinction for them, and for them to believe in it. After all, they can do almost anything, and they can do it faster than we adults.

We would want them to be excited about the notion of space exploration, medical breakthroughs, or even a transatlantic soccer match. These were distant realms for us when we were young, in the 1950s and 1960s, separate from the immediate worlds in which we dwelled. When we were children and we thought about such things, and when we saw such things on a television screen, our breath was taken away. There was a singular quality to the scientific and spiritual achievements that we absorbed as teenagers.

But where we had mystery, they have access—to sophisticated machinery, to sexual activity, to chemical substances, to guns. Now these busy children of the 1990s can simply dial such things up on coaxial converter panels. They can note or dismiss milestones as quickly as the video screen erases the increasingly inflated imagery of human suffering that comes across at flickering speeds and numbs the young soul perhaps in search of genuine awareness. What is truly hallowed in the world of today's youngster who is being bombarded by information (much of it meaningless) accumulating at a rate infinitely greater than that of all the information gathered by the Allies to win the Second World War?

Children are holy and are meant to be the products of human love. I daresay that holiness is fleeting in this culture of ours where high school students share hypodermic needles sometimes as often as they share ideas. When I was in high school, I used to give a girl flowers before a date. Now, my two daughters will be instructed to give a boy a condom. But I am going to spend less time regretting this change of conditions than I am on promoting the importance and the sanctity of good human relationships. Beyond the peer pressure, the rampant casualness of physical contact, the now deadly danger of sex, are still two living, needful, and feeling girls who are my children!

Like most parents coping in the new world of "significant others" and live-in arrangements, I still believe in the separate category of love, which is consecrated by commitment. If "Yeah, me!" is a statement, and if *one* is a number, it's a small number when totalled against the number of all-consuming relationships a contemporary youngster knows before ever knowing the poetry of a real romance.

I have been an adult influence around young people for many years and in many places: Schools, summer camps, community centers, and houses of worship. I have talked with children, argued with them, bandaged them, sung to them, and, God help me, I have buried them.

Young people are America's last natural resource, and they are not recyclable. They are vulnerable, curious, and they are so wonderfully resilient. I want them to feel hopeful and inspiring things, and I want them not to be smothered by information and cynicism. I want them to believe in the power of the numeral one in a civilization that is increasingly intolerant of the notion of a single human soul. I want to successfully parent my own two daughters in a culture that betrays some very dark, even destructive, tendencies. If the streets of our country offer fewer answers for children, I want their homes to be safe havens for their questions.

This book of dialogue for today's parents is the result of what I hear and feel. Our culture is neither soft nor gentle nor kind. It is hard, rough, and even predatory. Ask any parent: Do you feel your children are safe? Do you know what they are thinking? Ask any teacher: Do you feel that your students are contented, that they are filled with a sense of well-being? Do you believe that they really understand the world around them? Ask both parents and teachers: Aren't these children growing up too quickly? Aren't they being asked to cope with too much? Shouldn't they be children a little longer?

In preparing this book, I spoke to a cross-section of young people. I asked them to submit questions that they typically find themselves pondering, questions that they would like to discuss with their parents. The twenty-two chapter titles in this book are actual questions posed by teenagers, chosen from over one hundred that I collected.

Young people today have a lot of questions because they are simply being fed too much data, and too little truth. Too many people with too little knowledge are gaining too much access to the minds of too many children.

We have a full crew of print and electronic media hosts

who are sponsoring rhetoric, indulgence, and danger. I have been seeing strange things on television: People are throwing chairs and epithets at each other in broadcast studios. They are outraging each other on the radio, on call-in shows, in advice columns. Unlikely heroes and peculiar celebrities get the spotlight: James Earl Ray does a live remote from his prison cell in order to promote his book; convicted carjackers are consulted for tips on how to keep yourself from being mugged, slashed, or raped.

The world of total and instant information may be interesting and even useful, but it can be overwhelming for young people. In the last few years alone, we and our children have had total visual access to the mine explosions of the Saudi desert, the killing fields of Bosnia, the murdering streets of Los Angeles and so many other American places. We and they took in the public testimony of Professor Anita Hill, the sexual and commercial exploits of famous call girls, and the open testimony of several celebrated rape suspects. Now, in this totally video culture, kids have admittance to the horrifying photographs of President John F. Kennedy's lifeless countenance and his head wounds, all revealed at three dollars a movie rental. Is all of this access redeeming to our children? I doubt it. Does all of this lend urgency to their questions? I am sure of it.

We can perhaps sift through all of this, although not always. Sometimes, when my daughters walk into the room and I realize what is on television, I leap for the remote control. I want to shield their eyes, if I haven't my own. The television becomes a monstrous, intrusive box of horrors, bringing its noise, rancor, and meanness into our midst. I know that my daughters, Sari and Debra, like any

American youngsters, cannot be totally shielded from the real world. I know that they can be harmed by overprotection. But unless we couple their exposure to it with our willingness to discuss it, these innocent children may be left behind in the confusion of what we allow them to hear and see on the airwaves.

We were once the children. Our parents had the task of answering our questions about such things as living, loving, lying, leaving, learning, and limiting. Now we are the parents, and children look into our eyes for direction. Our parents may have had it easier, because the world then was less immediate. Now our children see more, hear more, know more, and, I truly believe, need more. We must talk with them while they are still willing to look back at us and listen. The rabbis understood a lot centuries ago when they declared, simply, that life is with people.

CHAPTER 1

Why Is the World So Scary?

"I feel paranoid," admits Katie, a fifteen-year-old girl who is a friend of my older daughter Sari. "I feel unsafe. Is it because of all the scary things I see on TV and in the movies? Do I know about too much of this bad stuff?"

The answer is, partially, yes. If you see frightening images, you may very well become frightened. If you see these images in vivid colors, and if you hear the accompanying noise delivered in stereo, you are likely to be especially frightened. If you continuously see and hear violence and death, then you become familiar with and affected by these things, and the awareness could make any youngster feel threatened.

However, the other part of the answer to the question "Why is the world so scary?" does not have to do with the current influx of video images that portray violence. It is also a general characteristic of teenagers to know about more than they can sometimes handle. They are too old to read children's books, and too young to comprehend much adult literature. And yet, in the course of their growing years, we ask them to know their religion, to exhibit good citizenship, and to be comprehensive in their answers to adults' questions. We ask them to live in a world of evil but fully expect them to be caring and good. So, while television does intrude, adolescent life itself brings with it a significant and natural amount of exploration and information gathering. "The world is too much with us," the rabbinic tradition declared—long before the mass media came along to amplify every already complicated aspect of growing up.

However, Katie carries a particular fear that breaks my heart: She quotes the statistics about how many women will be raped in this country, and she is often awakened from the recurring nightmare of her own "inevitable" rape. There may be some psychological factors at work here, but she is certainly getting the image of rape reinforced in fictional video settings and concretized by the nightly local news. She's intelligent and savvy; I believe that these qualities will help to protect her from making the wrong moves someday on a college campus or on any street. But her parents cannot dismiss her fears as being "just part of growing up."

The fears of this young girl are, in effect, listed in *TV Guide* and catalogued in the movie section of every American newspaper. So many productions are about the brutality that is carried out between people. Parents have to contend with the fact that evil has penetrated, through headphones, video monitors, and multiplex screens, directly into the minds and hearts of our impressionable children. Growing up was always many-faceted; now it is also vividly multichanneled.

The first thing we might do is to remember our own experience. Our teenagers are not the first generation of television watchers who are potentially affected by difficult images. It was our own generation, after all, that came into adolescence fully exposed, on a daily basis, to the televised reports of the Vietnam War. The nadir of our broadcasted incubus came in 1968, when the war and its endless casualty numbers were coupled with the terrifying accounts of successive assassinations, urban riots, and a disrupted, angry political convention. Many of us saw the terror in black and white, but we were well aware of the color of blood. Without question, we were forced to confront the issues of mortality and cruelty while we were still quite young and impressionable.

Like many parents my age now, I still remember the trembling voice of Senator Edward M. Kennedy as he eulogized his brother Robert in June 1968. The televised funeral both saddened and informed me. "Love is not an easy feeling to put into words," said the deeply bereaved brother. At the age of fifteen, I was scared and alarmed; I had worshipped both Robert Kennedy and Martin Luther King, Jr. Nonetheless, the same television set that had conveyed the agonizing scenes at the Ambassador Hotel in Los Angeles, where Robert Kennedy was murdered, now brought me the poignant insight spoken by Edward Kennedy in New York City. At fifteen, I knew very well that my country was in deep trouble. This knowledge gave me nightmares from time to time. But it also allowed me to participate in what my country was feeling on various levels.

I am grateful that my parents did not turn off the television in 1968, but even more grateful that they talked with me a great deal about what television had shown me. Today, my daughters see even more explicit images on their television, and the carnage, in full color, does not need imagination to help it deliver a powerful and brutal message. Therefore, I do what my parents did in talking about it as much as possible. The set is also turned off from time to time because it is increasingly evident that the violence being shown is gratuitous. There is not always something to talk about with Sari and Debra, and they do not need extra fuel for the bad dreams that are already somewhat inevitable at their ages.

Indeed, the intrusion of broadcast evil probably began on November 24, 1963. Perhaps that was the day when the collective innocence of our adolescent children was given a stark qualification forever. On that Sunday morning, while several million people (myself included) were watching on television, Jack Ruby lunged forward with a pistol and shot Lee Harvey Oswald in the abdomen. The images were grainy but not vague. It was the first occasion for what has since become a frequent happening: a murder presented on television. In some ways, it was more frightening then than it is now because in 1963 it was still unusual. Certainly, on that day, evil came home across the cathode ray of TV; it now is a permanent resident in our homes. We rent it, we turn it on with a remote-control button, we pay for it monthly as we send our checks to the cable company. What we need to also do is to account for it with our kids. We need to look, listen, and love.

No parent today should go more than a couple of days without asking his or her teenager what's been on television lately, and if there is anything worth talking about. There is hardly a bad time for dialogue in the home. If the published report is accurate that every American child will eventually see 100,000 acts of violence on television, then every parent should aspire to ask his or her child what he or she is thinking about at least that many times. If that seems unrealistic, we should at least consider how realistic the video images are that are filtering through to our children and making them sometimes feel vulnerable.

In discussing the television program, the movie, or the magazine article that has affected your child, you also have the opportunity to turn its effect in favor of knowledge. Television news, for example, is often criticized for being brazen, for utilizing our fears, and for just being downright exploitative. It's rather easy to raise this charge against the media; I myself have been prone to do it when I have seen something particularly outrageous. And yet, there have been some outrages shown on television that might have remained unchallenged had the media not brought them to our attention.

Many of us who are parents, teachers, and professionals try to teach our children about the ideas of human dignity, fairness, and equality. We want them to regard these principles with care and reverence. The question is, where did we in the older generation get such notions? Surely, they were taught to us by our own parents and conveyed to us in the history and social studies classes of the 1950s and

1960s. But the fact is that we learned the most about these subjects because the network news organizations saw fit to broadcast the civil rights revolution into our homes and collective consciousness. The conveyed dispatch of a policeman turning a high-pressure fire hose on a group of citizens protesting their inability to share a dining counter or a voting booth with other citizens was a defining, teaching moment for our generation. The inhumanity of racial segregation was not just curbed because people suddenly received some spiritual insight about it. To a great extent, it was confronted because enough people in enough places watching enough television sets were offended enough to demand the kind of federal legislation that was needed to stop it.

The same can be said about Vietnam: The youngsters who eventually stopped it were not the ones who had gone there to fight. They and their parents were the ones who saw it on television. Indeed, it must be remembered that the Indochina disaster was so painful for our society that motion pictures about it were not produced until years after the war finally ended. It was, specifically, the network news that brought the war to a halt. Our parents complained about the amount of horror that was shown from Saigon in those days, and they certainly sought to curtail our viewing of it. But without television, who would have known just how wrong and hopeless that war turned out to be?

We must be caring partners with our teenagers in the management of television, but we must not make blanket assumptions or value judgments, either. I certainly do not want Sari and Debra to watch murders night after night, but I do want them to be *aware* of the dangers that do exist for them every night. I don't want Sari's friend to have nocturnal terrors about being raped, but I absolutely want her to be informed enough on the topic so as to not grow up with any kind of naïveté. Where is the line drawn between exposure to the media and protection from them? In the end, every parent must go with his or her instincts and make such a decision with the children. Teenagers cannot be fooled or cajoled and they *must not* be patronized. But to do nothing about the reality of intrusive media imagery is to leave your youngster subject to the storms of the night.

Here are some suggested guidelines on how to answer the question, "Why is the world so scary?"

The first thing to remember is that if a child knows about things, a parent should regard the acquisition of knowledge itself as a positive. No teenager I have ever met wanted to be told that he or she shouldn't know about such-and-such; a youngster finds that type of response denigrating. They know about the issue because they were exposed to it; our job as parents is better handled by exploring it, not by denying it. If we try to just turn off the issue, the youngster will first feel humiliated and will then go talk about it with someone else. I'd rather manage my daughters' fears myself than have another youngster, another adult who I don't necessarily know, or another television program do it for me.

One thing not to do, when watching something upsetting on television with a child, is to start criticizing or bemoaning our country and our society just for the emotional satisfaction of doing it. Kids are unnerved when they hear their parents react in this way; the subject of violence, for example, is frightening enough. Wanton comments about this being "a sick country" or about the racial backgrounds of people shown on television do little for youngsters but reinforce their fears or their prejudices. Don't rationalize anything, but do discuss it. As a parent you also have the right and the responsibility to make your views known to your child, and to reassure him or her that, in a world so affected by hate and upheaval, you are there with your insights and with your love.

Your teenager is more interested in exchanging ideas and values with you about what's happening in the world than in just letting the videos describe it. Now is the time, and we might even draw upon a very modern image with which to offer the most important suggestion in this matter: Let there be a private channel, always clicked on, between you and your child. Keep your eyes and ears open, and your heart tuned in.

CHAPTER 2

❦

How Old Should I Be
to Have Sex?

If your son or daughter hasn't asked you this yet, you can nonetheless be reasonably sure that he or she has been pursuing the question elsewhere. Sexual activity is now in the province of children. We hear about twelve-year-old girls who are pregnant; we have become aware of a whole segment of American society in which grandmothers are raising babies on behalf of a generation of pubescent parents who have abandoned their responsibilities, who cannot handle the situation, or who have simply vanished.

Grandparents raising their grandchildren is not quite mainstream yet, but children having sexual encounters is not unusual at all. I am amazed sometimes by the surprised reactions of some parents when they learn that their teen-aged children are, in fact, sexually active. There is a real knowledge gap here; parents watch children on television and in movies experiencing remarkable things. Yet these same parents are never imagining that their own children are out there, watching the same images, being influenced by and sometimes participating in life's experiments and adventures.

But before dealing with the above question, you might want to consider the question of how and why this new scenario came about.

I remember reading a newspaper headline recently that announced the birth of a child to prominent and wealthy New York real estate developer Donald Trump and his celebrity girlfriend, Marla Maples. The birth was heralded in social circles, and there was a fair amount of speculation about what the baby would mean to mother, father, and their circle of friends and acquaintances.

The fact that the two parents were not yet married to each other was not a focus of the article. Nor are unwed parents particularly uncommon; we have even modified our language to accommodate the new leniency. People refer to each other as "significant others" in good times while suing each other for palimony at other times that are not so good.

I recall seeing a recent, popular television program called *Wings*. The episode, as always, was filled with attractive, athletic young men and women who wore beautiful clothing and who flashed significant sexual body language among each other. One of the leading men was having a difficult time telling his buddy about a bewildering situation he had just encountered. It was painful for him to admit this disappointing fact, but he had just had sex with his girlfriend and, well, it just wasn't as exciting as he would have desired.

The program was being telecast at 8:30 in the evening. Most youngsters were quite awake at that hour and would become part of the innocent audience laughter reacting to the poor guy's predicament. It occurred to me, as I turned the set off, that the frustrated gentleman was no longer part of a culture that even presumes that people who have sex with each other (and apparently have a need to evaluate it with others) are married to each other. This may be a form of progress, but I can't imagine any thoughtful woman agreeing that such dialogue is progressive.

So be it. What adults do to and with each other, and what other adults want to see, hear, or read concerning all of this is not the subject of my concerns here. What I am concerned about is the effect of all this on the minds and bodies of youngsters who are capable of creating babies, who have totally natural yearnings about lovemaking, but who are usually not as emotionally equipped as the magazine covers, movies, and cologne commercials are telling them they are.

We have a society that appears to be generally permissive, but parents are still in charge of granting kids most kinds of specific permission. The advertising moguls who are placing suggestive photographs of men and women into everyday newspapers and magazines, and who run soft-core pornography on general access cable stations probably do not think about the moral equations involved. I'm not sure that they have to; nor is America's morality under examination here. But American children, in effect, are. Standards change in all civilizations. Even the Bible has a wide and inconsistent pattern of sexual behavior. Abraham, the founding father of Judaism, kept and discarded concubines. David, the king and poet, had to have young women brought to him when he was old and dispirited, because he could not keep himself warm.

Meanwhile, kids continue to be born with the same chemical attributes, physiological circumstances, and hormones that have characterized human beings since the beginning. As parents and professionals, we must recognize this and consider this reality in terms of the times in which we live.

A young man is not automatically equipped to discern Donald Trump's personal behavior as a father or a husband just because the youngster lives in the 1990s. A young woman does not have insight about how to manage and safeguard her body in the era of Madonna just because she attends high school in this era. But when we were the children, the private lives and anatomies of celebrities were not so readily available to us, and the parents of our television families were unquestionably married to each other and, yes, were portrayed as sleeping in separate beds. The subject of sex was undoubtedly shrouded, and probably repressed. Innocence lingered, as did a certain level of ignorance about things that really do matter to parents and their adolescent children.

It is hard to say which generation—ours or that of our children—has really been better off. But it is not hard at all to say which generation is coping with more information, vividness and, above all, pressure. Let's be less judgmental with our children and more helpful.

Let's also be honest. Do we think that it's easy to be fourteen or fifteen years old these days? When we were sexually busy in the Woodstock era, we were still inhibited by certain norms and realities. Who was able to wear such bold and unduly flattering clothing to junior high school? Who was able to bring the music right into the school via headphones, portable quadrophonic units, and rechargeable micro-television sets? Who smelled as good as these young women, had such smooth hands, red lips, and as much jewelry? Who is also the first generation to know, categorically, that their parents were the graduates of the original era as much celebrated for its sexual liberation as its flirtation with civil rights?

These children of the 1990s are fast, sophisticated, and they are not stupid. Whatever they didn't know about last week will be available to them next week on Fox, CNN, or VH-1. We may still be wondering about how to explain sexual relations to them, but at their school, somebody we assigned or elected to educational responsibilities may have already given them the instructions, the warnings, and perhaps even a condom to go with it.

It's time that we look, listen, and love.

I don't think that the thing to do is to wait for your son or daughter to ask you about sex. Asking *them* about it, at a time that just seems right, can do a lot for your ability to engage in dialogue together. It also gives you the opportunity to acknowledge their unquestionable awareness of a subject that is as much on your child's mind as it is on yours. One assumes that most parents want their growing children to have all the right and healthy working parts, and that parents wish upon their offspring the eventual joy and pleasure of sex—in the appropriate, safe, and timely settings.

Teenagers want you to acknowledge their feelings about special friends. It is good to talk with them, especially at a time when there *isn't* a crisis atmosphere. Better to broach sexual relations as part of a general discussion than after word has arrived of an unwanted and untimely pregnancy.

"You really care about him, don't you?" This is generally a welcome and appropriate inquiry of a daughter who is experiencing the fresh, exhilarating, and sometimes overwhelming reality of adolescent love. It is also a good way to expand the conversation, and with that, your relationship with your maturing youngster. There is nothing wrong with asking your child if there is respect in his or her relationship with another person.

"Are you careful about sex?" This is a legitimate question. Spoken in the right tone, it only indicates that you care, not that you are prying.

"We are not having sex," may be the response. If you believe your child, then you should encourage him or her that such abstinence is not only rare (your teenager will probably tell *you* that), but very sensible in this day and age. "I want you two to have great times together" is a very good thing to tell your youngster. He or she just wants your approval of the friend and your understanding of these new, fluttering emotions that he or she is experiencing. Teenagers are going to become emotionally involved no matter what we would wish. The best way to keep their confidence, and therefore gain some influence over their eventual physical decisions, is to offer a smiling and warm attitude about the friend—as long as he or she is a tolerable individual. This is not likely to be your eventual son- or daughter-in-law.

If, however, the answer you get is something to the effect that "it's none of your business if we're having sex," then your firm response should unabashedly be that it definitely is your business. The consequences to your child's medical health or to the welfare of a sudden newborn baby that nobody is equipped to handle compels all parties in such a dialogue to cut to the chase: "Look," you might say, "I can't be there to prevent you from having sex with someone you shouldn't be doing it with. But I can tell you that I want to trust you. If you go ahead and do it, then you know that you will be breaking our trust, and you will be making a mistake that can rob you of many great years. Just don't do it! Enjoy your relationship, but just don't have sex, because I'm your parent and I have to tell you that it would be a serious mistake, plain and simple." There is simply no reason in the world—especially this crazy world—for a responsible parent to soft-pedal the dangers of teenage sex to the very teenager a parent is raising.

If you are nervous about giving them answers, just imagine how terrifying it is for them to ask the questions. If you are offended by the question, consider this: Thinking about sex and having sex are not necessarily the same things. A child who is curious is a child who is alive. Be fair and patient with the creation that passed through you and now has the same longings that you did before everything supposedly made perfect sense in your time and place.

When a teenager asks the question, "How old should I

be to have sex?" she may also be telling you that she is experiencing a new set of feelings for somebody. This question is not necessarily the report of a budding nymphomaniac, nor is it an implied threat of some kind. It should be regarded as an invitation to talk about something very personal and very important. A parent who regards it as a real opportunity is bound to accomplish something positive with his or her child.

Rebecca is a young woman I know who has a problem. She is pretty, outgoing, and a favorite of the boys in her high school. She told me some time ago, when she was in ninth grade, that her parents constantly inquired about her private life. "It's none of their business," she complained.

"But Rebecca," I said, "they are your parents. Don't they have a right to know about what's happening?"

"They only ask me about sex. They never ask me about anything else. They don't bug me about what's going on in my classes, if I'm feeling good, if I have any friends. Except if my friends are boys. And do I give myself away to them. The only time my father even asks me about how I'm doing in general is if I'm in a bad mood—or what he calls a bad mood—and he's wondering if I'm having my period. My period is what he's worried about. He doesn't care about anything in my life, but when it comes to my period and my body and boys, he just won't leave me alone. Well, since he has no respect for my privacy, I'm not going to tell him anything about myself."

Rebecca breaks my heart because she is too young for such sexual anxiety and she likely is being sexually active—on one level to punish her parents for their rather uneven interest in her life. I think parents should ask their children about personal matters, but in a manner that indicates a certain level of discretion and, yes, respect. Confronting a girl about her menstrual flow in the manner described above is degrading, insulting, and counterproductive. At the very least, Rebecca's parents are betraying a lot of paranoia to their troubled little girl. Tremendous walls are going up between child and parents. No wonder Rebecca feels no compunction about having sexual relations. She probably wants her parents to be nearby, although not too close. That's the complicated nature of adolescent life in a civilization that is so open and brazen that all kids have left are parents to balance matters of discipline and privacy.

I was taking a walk once with my older daughter, Sari, who was thirteen years old at the time. We were chatting away about people we know, about school, the weather, and the kind of world we live in. Like any parent, I was feeling a rush of pride in this emerging and interesting youngster who I noticed has a delicious sense of humor. A quiet intimacy prevailed along the walk, so I decided to ask my daughter something about herself.

"Sari, do you know how to make a baby?"

"Yes, Dad."

"Good. So don't."

Of course, Sari laughed at my impulsive comment, but the subject was effectively broached. In my case, there was nothing further to be said at that moment; in your case, in your house, on your walk, it may be different. What is never different is the need for parents and children not to pretend that the world is not turning.

"Good, so don't" is not a full answer, nor will it suffice

indefinitely. But when a youngster is discussing sex, we don't have to produce a formulaic, all-encompassing response or manifesto that will clarify or neutralize all the issues. The two people, father and daughter, who were taking a nice walk that particular evening will not be exactly the same two people who will need to talk about it again. Sari may not always get the right answer—or the one she wants me to offer. But she will always get access to what I'm thinking, and I'll try to do the best I can.

I think it's fair and reasonable for a teenager to be responsible to his or her feelings and urges. When you tell your son or daughter that he or she is not old enough yet to have sexual relations, you have every right to tell the whole story: Sex is not necessarily satisfying, it is not always as rich as the emotions two young people believe they carry for each other. It is simply not always the right course. Tell them, don't hide! There are also, of course, urgent matters of safety and welfare—to be discussed specifically in the third chapter of this book.

"Don't give yourself away," I've admonished Sari in later discussions, hoping and praying that the trust we have in each other—built up over layers of time—will service her when she finds herself in a real quandary. I think she does not resent my admonitions because I have not offered them while prying and I have stated my concerns as well in a number of other important categories besides sex.

Some people who read this approach may become very impatient with me. There are those who believe that the only way to protect a child's morals is to absolutely impose moral authority upon that child. "You will not have intercourse with anybody until you are married." "If you get pregnant, I will throw you out on the street."

If such a tack works, then I salute the parent involved. I haven't seen it work very well over the years. I have had a lot of youngsters, who really weren't such bad types, come to me guilt-ridden, frustrated, even estranged from parents whose eyes bulged with anger, whose voices rocked with anxiety before anybody even started listening to each other in the house. I daresay that, in this open and ripe era of commercialism and Nielsen ratings, self-righteousness produces a lot of noise at home but not too much understanding. Rather than threatening a child with the door, it might be better to open the door to yourself.

In the end, a teenager will probably decide for himself when he is old enough to have sex. If we are lucky, he'll make his decision in sync with what we parents would wish. However, a bit of discretion, and a lot of genuine interest in the life of your child will guarantee at least your emotional participation in his or her very real struggle.

Tell your kids what you think, and be honest about how it was a generation ago. Don't make up stories, and don't rely on Scripture for this one. Your son or daughter's body and everybody's peace of mind are all truly at stake now, in this life. And don't ever tire of telling your teenager how wonderful love is when it has more to do with the upper parts of the body than the lower.

CHAPTER 3

Do I Have to Worry
About AIDS?

Some of God's miracles would not be allowed to take place these days—because of state and federal health regulations. AIDS has changed everything; it's in the blood of civilization.

I am thinking of the Passover seder, when participants recall the very frightening tenth plague. According to the biblical story, all of Egypt's firstborn sons were destroyed. How did the Angel of Death know which houses contained Egyptian children in this dark and troubling story? Specifically, how did the angel know to "pass over" the homes of Hebrew families?

The Hebrews were instructed to mark their doors with fresh blood. This would signal the Angel of Death to avoid their dwellings. Granted, the blood came from butchered lambs, but in the process of slaughtering, human blood could have easily mixed in. There were no guidelines then from the provincial Department of Agriculture, no rubber gloves, no face masks, no HIV virus.

Such a forced compression of blood and flesh could not have been mandated by a caring God in an era of Acquired Immune Deficiency Syndrome. I spell out the phrase because some people don't even know anymore what AIDS stands for. But most adults, and most kids, know that AIDS is a very real plague that spells trouble.

The Angel of Death that floats over society these days would laugh to itself if confronted with bloodstains across the doorways of our dwellings, our hospitals, our prisons. The irony would not be lost upon such a sinister angel; blood is the one thing, our teenagers are taught in STD (sexually transmitted diseases) classes that may be the cause —and not the prevention—of the death of children. Nor does any death angel discriminate anymore among Hebrew, Egyptian or any nationality of children.

AIDS is here, now, everywhere. It has seeped into the mind-set and worries of young people like the fourteen-year-old boy who asked the question that titles this chapter. Lennie is a soft-spoken boy with big eyes and a healthy amount of freckles. He is one of the few fourteen year olds I know who still looks like a fourteen year old. His question, set against the hope he has of enjoying sex one day, is both terrifying and poignant. It is a paradigm of the kind of world our children live in. It gives us both an informed sense of what these teenagers know, and, admittedly, an opportunity to save some of them from both gratuitous sexual activity and possible death.

On one hand, Lennie's parents might be upset that he

contemplates having sex. A lot of parents seem possessed of this anxiety; this is understandable and normal. Most things that our teenagers say or do make us feel older than we wish to feel! When I blessed Lennie at his bar mitzvah ceremony, for example, his parents wept. They are a close and gentle family. The tears parents experience at such tender moments have as much to do with the achievements of their children as with the bittersweet acknowledgement that life is advancing—at a faster pace than we would care to admit. The tears we wipe at milestones are the salty waters of growth and insight.

Most of us don't want our kids to be old enough to plan for sexual activity. We resent the closing in of time and circumstance. We become angry at all the outside pressures and influences, such as the media, that dazzle our children with promises and challenges. We don't want Lennie and all the others to know so much. But I daresay that we want those same sources to let Lennie know as much as possible about the reality of AIDS in this civilization.

We can't have it both ways. Sex may be stayed; AIDS is already here to stay. It's killing people from all walks of life and Lennie's question is one of the most important questions that I hope your child is asking as well. In spite of a pervasive denial that I detect in the basically suburban and affluent community that I serve as rabbi, AIDS is not an affliction confined to the gay or creative or fringe communities. I certainly knew that on the day I buried a nice Jewish doctor who died of this disease.

Stuart was an accomplished physician whose family simply does not fit the stereotype we obsessively associate with the HIV virus. His father is a thoughtful man, possessed of much philosophical strength as well as very observant re-ligious habits. Clearly, the Jewish God had not steered the Angel of Death away from this family: Stuart's father had already buried his wife and one of his two daughters some time before Stuart died of what used to be called the "gay cancer." The two women, whose headstones awaited us at the cemetery the day we came to bury Stuart, had died of other causes. AIDS is no peripheral business; it mixes into the soil of memory right along with all the other reasons people die in our times.

I myself felt a certain incredulity at the time Stuart's one surviving sister phoned me with the news of his death. It was a few years ago, but I still hadn't dealt directly, as the officiating rabbi, with such a circumstance. (I do not lack for opportunities anymore; Lennie's piercing question underscores the point.) But up to the time of the young doctor's tragedy, I had personally associated AIDS with the theatre—where my family has many friendship roots, and where many have indeed become absent friends.

As in so many categories, the acting community has guided us to a better awareness of something that churns within our society. My working friends on stage have been attending a lot of funerals for quite a few years now. The rest of us ought to take note of this, not only because we have a moral obligation, but because many of our children who now live with us in the safer cubicles of suburban developments carry very vivid dreams of making it as lyri-cists, dramatists, singers, dancers, and actors. There is more risk to them now than just a casting director's rejection slip.

Success in the arts (or any other field) is no guarantee of immunity, either. This came home vividly for me and a gathered audience one recent evening when the renowned contemporary composer Alan Menken performed a concert of his compositions during a visit to his synagogue in greater New York.

Mr. Menken chose a selection of songs from his recently released feature, *Beauty and the Beast*. He introduced some pieces from another animated musical of his that was then forthcoming, *Aladdin*. Alan Menken is successful, happily married, famous, and bereaved. Through much of the evening in that temple, he spoke tenderly about his departed collaborator in composition, Howard Ashman. Ashman had died a few months earlier from AIDS. Menken's continuous elegy was a mixture of love and anguish.

I remember the great melodies that were heard that evening, and the excitement of being close to a true creative genius and his family. But I remember better the realization: AIDS, again, robbed us of music, poetry, drama, and friendship. It has taken us all a few years, but we seem to finally understand that it is a plague that is robbing us of real people who live next door and who lie in the same cemeteries as our neighbors, our siblings, our teachers, our doctors.

Lennie's question about sex and AIDS is less about exploration and more about fear. We have to consider how scary it is to be a teenager in this day and age. When we were either testing our parents with questions about sex, or actually experimenting with it, we were concerned with proprieties, with being found out, with pregnancy, and, yes, with certain diseases that had serious consequences. Syphilis and gonorrhea were and remain significant infections, and it was a good thing for us to learn and understand just how vulnerable we could become if we were reckless with our bodies. It was appropriate and timely for us to hear in junior high school about the genitourinary tract, about the rectum and cervix, about the dangers caused by gonococci following sexual intercourse.

If all this was right a generation ago, it's even more evident now that sex education is critical for youngsters as early as in the seventh grade. Most parents are satisfied that their teenagers are studying STDs in school. Most parents are relieved when their children take a field trip to the local health museum and learn about the HIV virus from a set of charts, graphics, and videos provided on display. And yet many parents will still never discuss the matter at home—when the life at stake is the very child we most want to protect in the world.

It would seem redundant to mention to parents, as the twentieth century draws to a close, that AIDS remains a significant retrovirus that a child can acquire from a tainted blood transfusion (in spite of heroic efforts by the medical community to control the blood supply), from the use of unsanitary drug paraphernalia, or from sexual contact with a person already carrying the virus. We can dismiss it as an ailment of certain class groupings or we can disdain it as some kind of divine retribution sent to earth because of sinful or wayward behavior on the part of people we don't know or like. Having worked out our own anxieties and phobias in this manner, we are still left with the fact that a lot of very fine teenagers who hope to have fulfilling sexual lives someday (preferably with monogamous partners) feel possibly cheated and definitely scared.

You need to talk about AIDS at home with your child. Don't leave the safety instructions, or the bold disclaimers about how small the odds are of getting AIDS, to the state or federal governments that collect your taxes but don't raise your kids. I am reminded of a fairly recent announcement made by the government, in conjunction with yet another university research project, that margarine is not so good for us, after all. First it was the perfect, low-fat alternative to butter; now it contains a sinister amount of hidden fatty acids that are actually dangerously counter-productive. One day the government tells us that calcium is wonderful, the next day it's not so sure. Canada hates saccharin, the United States hates cyclamates, neither side is really sure what's killing the laboratory rats. Thirty years after it had evidence that nicotine is addictive, the govern-ment decides (thankfully) to release a barrage of pro-nouncements against the tobacco industry.

We *can't* depend on the official decrees that, really, the chances of a youngster contracting the HIV virus are min-iscule. If the government can't make up its mind about breakfast spreads and sweeteners, why is it so certain about a blood infection that is actually spreading rather dramat-ically among the heterosexual population of this country? Certainly we get useful guidelines and warnings from po-litical and medical bureaucrats about how to prevent the possibility of AIDS. Certainly we acknowledge, with mea-surable and understandable discomfort, that the use of con-doms in our society is a necessary safeguard in the war against this plague.

But this issue is not to be ultimately negotiated on a subway advertisement, a television commercial or in a newspaper announcement. It is required material in a responsible school, but it must first be heard about right at home. At the very least, this dramatic and harrowing topic of discussion will certainly prove or disprove the level of communication really happening between you and your child.

If you resent this whole business of condoms, then you should tell your child to choose a life of sexual abstinence until marriage. While none of us is immune from disease, abstinence does at least significantly lower the odds against exposure to the HIV virus. So, in talking with your kids, and weighing your own family values about sexual behavior, at least make a pitch in favor of a full emotional commitment before a physical concession! Society certainly is not doing that; it is passing out condoms in schools and sterilized hypodermic needles in the streets. Do I think that all of this is a good idea? Probably. We are in so deep in terms of social malaise that such measures are likely beneficial as public health precautions. But I don't want to concede the health of my child and yours to a public policy born more of necessity than of moral persuasion.

It's good that Lennie and other kids fear the consequences of sexual activity in such an era. We have a right to carefully exploit these fears—not at the expense of any cultural groups, but in favor of the welfare of the children assigned to us. And when a teenager asks how you can preach abstention when you did not wait for marriage before having sex, give that teenager the kind of direct answer I once heard a very fine mother give her teenage daughter as they both sat before me in my office:

"There was a lot less at stake for me! If there had been

a virus like this back then," the mother pleaded, gripping her daughter's hands and peering directly into her child's tear-stained eyes, "would you have even asked me about the moral implications of the whole thing?! Maybe sex was wrong then, but as far as we knew, it was safe. I don't want you to possibly get a terrible disease for the pleasure of a few moments."

I think I was privy to a moment of absolute, even anguished, honesty between a parent and a child at that instant. Every ailment, every disease, every abuse stands threatened, in one degree or another, when parents and children mingle souls.

Sure, it's hard for a youngster to comprehend any danger to himself. Life at fifteen or sixteen seems limitless. Characters having sexual encounters on television and in the movies are athletic and remarkably cool. Who thinks about death and dying when the whole world seems to lay at our feet? Express your understanding of all this to your child, and encourage him to recognize that you are asking for abstinence because you want him to experience just that very expanse of unlimited life and love.

From time to time, I receive a note from a nearby church in my community about a walk-in clinic called the Open House. Clergy of various faiths meet in support of this special place because, regardless of ethnic or social standing, every congregation "has AIDS" and must offer education and services to victims and their close ones. The Open House offers and arranges for transportation, hospital visitations, food and housekeeping help, and just plain care. People volunteer to come and talk to patients; there are small acts of kindness that serve to defer the loneliness that is as insidious as the infection. I believe that even the inevitable Angel of Death is moved enough to at least pause in the doorways of these fading human lives.

After the young doctor Stuart died, it was his sister Gail who moved to create the Open House. Working with a Catholic nun, this sweet and sorrowful wife and mother turned her grief into a working compassion that should inspire any contemporary family to generally reconsider its own priorities.

Whenever possible, I encourage the teenage youngsters of my synagogue to go over and volunteer some time at the Open House. Most of them don't; they're scared, and their parents are somewhat paranoid about such an exposure. I am not judgmental about this. A few of the kids have gone, however. I have no doubt that these precious few are now less likely to give away their bodies or challenge any angels.

CHAPTER 4

When Is the Right Time
for Me to Start Drinking?

Kids are drinking. Alcohol, like marijuana or cocaine, is but one of the drugs that is seducing and harming young people. A parent who believes that if his or her teenager keeps away from hard drugs, then he or she is not flirting (or worse) with alcohol is a parent who may be operating with illusions. Unfortunately, there is a social tension surrounding the use of alcohol; I see it even in the synagogue.

Every Saturday morning, just after completing the sabbath service and the accompanying bar or bat mitzvah ceremony, I stand behind a large table just outside the chapel of my synagogue. Before me, typically, is an ornate and twisted loaf of bread called *challah*. The bread will be blessed and shared in honor of the happy occasion of a youngster experiencing a true milestone.

To the right and left of the bread are glass cups, one side containing grape juice and the other, wine. Either choice is acceptable religiously at the moment; the blessing we make thanks God for creating "the fruit of the vine."

But I don't always enjoy these moments by the table. I do wave the bread knife jokingly in the air, admonishing the teenagers present that "I'm watching every move." Regardless of my good-natured security measure, some youngster or two surely manages to get his or her adolescent lips on the alcoholic fruit of the vine.

We are told that alcohol consumption is down in our country. The trend has been documented by enough sources to suggest that it's true. There has been a reported and significant decline in the number of highway fatalities attributable to the abuse of alcohol, as more and more people are acquiescing to a designated driver or just a cutback in their own intake. All of this should help a parent to tell a youngster that the right time to start drinking is never when one has any kind of responsibility for any other human being.

But teenage kids are drinking, sometimes quite a lot. As such, I watch the celebrating teenagers who gather around me at the blessing over the wine in the temple, at wedding feasts or other such occasions when the general elation of the crowd somewhat blurs the need to keep kids aware of the sweet alcohol. The kids who are thirteen or fourteen eye each other nervously; their adolescent body language betrays the inherent peer pressure in this awkward moment that mixes the holy with the social.

It's not that I think that a sip of grape wine is going to destroy a youngster. As rabbi, I actually hand the wine goblet to the newly blessed thirteen year old as we conclude the bar mitzvah service with a sung consecration. The warm and syrupy drink tickling the throat helps to mark the happy passage. There is no religious metaphor here; the wine represents nothing except the joy of the day.

However, at such a moment the alcoholic drink is connected to some responsibility, some context of meaning. Nobody is just "drinking." Neither the youngster nor his parents are asked to share a throwaway libation devoid of any association with their own lives. Moreover, those who prefer grape juice in their cups of life are, of course, granted their request.

At such a moment, in the middle of a religious ceremony, we are light years away from the jittery, sophomoric exchange of bravado occurring around the wineglasses just after such ceremonies. A glass of wine shared when people are marking critical moments can be the "right time." It is a far cry from the dispersal of a case of beer in and around a convertible or a bag-concealed fifth of whiskey smuggled into a baseball game or into somebody's life who really is not prepared or old enough to handle the consequences. The question of when the right time is for drinking has as much to do with the setting as it does with someone's age.

When parents ask me about kids and alcohol, I ask them to consider their own drinking habits. When the bar in the house is central to a family's culture, then it is much easier for a teenager to succumb to peer pressure that occurs at an outside party, after school or at a friend's house that also has an ample bar setup. I have often seen homes where a mom or dad, hosting a Sunday gathering to watch a football game, actually employ the services of their son or daughter to mix and serve drinks to guests. I suppose some kids can handle this very direct exposure to vermouth, vodka, and bourbon without too much danger. But there is a creeping quality of the socially innocent to such afternoon or evening huddles. Somewhere, amidst the constellation of ice cubes, soda water, and hard liquor, a youngster may get the idea that all of this jocularity is really kind of inviting.

Since many of us adults drink, and some of us drink poorly or loudly, it may be somewhat pretentious to arbitrarily lay down any firm rules about teenage drinking. It is easier to deal with this subject when our own drinking is either limited, controlled, or just not so apparent to a youngster. Consider, however, that if you drink a lot, your teenager is going to basically realize it. Certainly any drinking on our part in conjunction with driving obviates any moral prerogative that we might wish to expend. Kids watch, kids note, kids sometimes drink.

While alcohol does appear to be a particularly major concern to teenagers today (marijuana and other drugs are understood to be potentially even more dangerous), and while many youngsters do sympathize with such groups as Students Against Drunk Driving (SADD) and Alcoholics Anonymous (AA), there are definitely kids who just drink. The question that titles this chapter is the barometer of a social issue that is undoubtedly on the agenda of junior and senior high school circles. I have found over the years that the abuse of alcohol, however, is sometimes less a matter of peer pressure than it is one of family function.

Most of the kids in my community who know a fifteen year old named Eric do not exalt his legendary drinking.

Eric arrives at most parties a little intoxicated and his problems increase with the night. "He seems so lonely," says one girl, who is truly worried about her classmate.

I understand that Eric's father is a bona fide alcoholic who refuses help and who drinks alone in the house.

We usually associate solo drinking with a dire, adult situation. When teenagers drink, they usually do so in groups and in response to each other's social challenges. But Eric, who is too young to drive or vote, drinks all by himself in the house. The reasons for his situation are best sifted through by a professional therapist, but it is not hard to conclude that the cause of this immense tragedy has something to do with a dangerous amount of self-contempt. It is hard to imagine a greater loneliness than that of a fifteen year old who opens a bottle of Scotch and drinks it with only his sadness. Maybe Eric's partnership with alcohol started when his parents had him wait on their dinner guests who desired cocktails. Certainly there has been alcohol in the home, and a very visible consumption of it by a parent who exemplifies the addiction and the isolation. Eric's father, likely a good man with his own set of real problems, is nonetheless an accessory in the murder of his son's spirit and body.

This is an extreme case, but the drink pours out of the bottle rather quickly. A parent must truly evaluate his own relationship to alcohol; is it really as benign as we assume? Meanwhile, each of us can likely recall someone from our own high school days who never made it to graduation because of some alcohol-related misfortune. To some degree or another, we drank when we were teenagers. In fact, our generation died from this affliction at a much higher rate

than today's teenage generation. Nor were there such public efforts made, by school districts, awareness groups, and
even by commercial broadcast stations, to dramatize the
effects of drunken driving and the appropriateness of abstention. In the end, this question has a lot to do with the
issue of personal responsibility.

"I am responsible for you," you should tell your teenager, "but I cannot be everywhere. You are responsible for
yourself most of the time."

"I can take care of myself," is a likely retort you will
get from a child brimming with annoyance. That's when a
clear discussion about the effects of alcohol consumption
on the human bloodstream and on the brain is in order.
Youngsters may appear to resent such a discussion, but they
really do want to know that we care about them and their
safety. There is a certain amount of peer pressure lurking
in the exasperation of a teenager at this parent's "interfer-
ence," but there is a lot more satisfaction in knowing that
there is parental love.

Meanwhile, alcohol abuse compromises the safety of
more than just the teenager on hand. If a young person
wants the privilege of driving an automobile as early as
sixteen or seventeen, then he or she must absolutely accept
the immense responsibility for others that comes with being a driver. If the state law is good enough to grant a kid
a driver's license at sixteen, then the other law requiring
that he be twenty-one in order to purchase liquor is also
good enough. Tell your growing adolescent this, and indi-
cate that this is more than a personal matter. It's a legal
matter that involves the ultimate responsibility people have
for each other, especially a parent for a child.

"When is the right time for me to start drinking?" The answer begins with the following correction in the child's thinking: Drinking is not a required social custom at all. Not to drink socially is a perfectly appropriate and very healthy option. Beyond that, the age of twenty-one, when kids do become adults in the civic sense, is a reasonable age to ask young people to consider as a line of demarcation. But I think a parent should ask a youngster to realize that the best time to start drinking is when you're old enough to understand that nobody who was ever healthy ever really needed a drink.

CHAPTER 5

Why Do People
Kill Each Other?

At a Taco Bell restaurant in the southeast corner of Indianapolis, a disgruntled customer opened fire after not receiving the order he requested. . . .

Outside the Wal-Mart, people rushed for cover as the gunman . . .

. . . when finally three of the commuter passengers were able to subdue the assailant who had already killed several people on the Long Island Railroad car.

The stray bullet struck the father in the head as his wife and two young children looked on. The shots were fired from a nearby mall escalator and were apparently part of a gang confrontation.

A youngster who is not asking the above question is a youngster who needs to hear from his or her parents. It is impossible for a teenager not to be thinking about this; in fact, it is likely that he or she is carrying a fair amount of anxiety on the subject. Today's children are not watching grainy serials about cowboys and Indians. They are watching videos of people blowing each other's brains out. They are seeing and hearing about so much murder that my greatest concern as a professional is that they may become too anesthetized to even ask the question, "Why do people kill each other?"

It should be understood that the question of why people kill each other existed long before the current debate in America about gun control and that the question will likely be around as long as there are people to kill each other. This may be a useful perspective in responding to your child's question. In other words, it is a sad fact that people have always hurt each other; the first "recorded" murder involved Cain and Abel of the Bible. Cain didn't pack a handgun, but he did pack human nature.

(In stating this, I am not, however, subscribing to the widely quoted notion that guns don't kill people but that people do. The preponderance of guns in our society is a terrifying factor in today's crime rate, and without question most teenagers fear guns and should reject any romanticizing of revolvers, rifles, and other weaponry.)

A recent curiosity was a major FBI report that violent crime was actually statistically declining in our country. Most kids I speak to have not actually believed the report and wonder how such an assertion could be made when they endure so much conveyed carnage through the media. It certainly *seems* like the violence is out of control, even if the ever-growing influence of the media helps to create the impression. But statistics aside, parents and their children live with a new level of concern and, hopefully, a heightened awareness for everybody's safety and well-being. If a child wonders why people kill each other, we should certainly include a healthy dose of common sense and useful behavior guidelines to go along with any psychological theories.

"You need to have a group go with you to the mall, and a definite and established meeting place at a specific time so that we can collect you" is as important a statement as any treatise on why some people are angry at society. Protect and supervise your children when they are out; give them a social studies lesson when they are home, safe with you.

"Yes, let's talk about this," you should say to your child when the subject of violence comes up. "Let's also figure out together how to be smart wherever we go and whenever we are in different places." You, the parent, should also be very declarative in establishing new and stricter rules about which places to visit, which friends to go out with, and what kind of curfew will be enforced because you surely mean it when you tell your child "I love you."

But some discussion of why human beings act the way we do is in order here. Teenagers, who undoubtedly see or even find themselves participating in unseemly or unkind acts from day to day, are quite aware of the less noble aspects of human behavior. Judaism firmly believes that every human being is born with two inclinations: For evil and for good. In the important tension between the two is the possibility for a lot of knowledge.

I think that we need to remind our youngsters that all people are prone to tawdriness, even if most do not commit major crimes. There is some truth to the ongoing complaint in our civilization that newspapers and television stations dwell on the bad news. There is also some truth to the media's retort that most people would not find the news interesting if it were not focused on the more sensational, if upsetting, trends in society.

From Cain and Abel to Oprah and Geraldo, human beings dwell on what human beings can and will do to each other. The world didn't start being evil in this decade; it just became more satellite connected. If our parents' generation had had as much broadcast access, day to day, to World War II as our children have now to some aspects of urban America, there would have been even more of a general gloom in 1944 than there was in 1994 about violence and inhumanity. Indeed, if CNN could have interviewed Adolf Hitler from his Berlin bunker, it would have. Accordingly, either the dictator's suicide would have been telecast live, or, better yet, both he and his heinous crimes would have been exposed earlier to a world that could have been spared both.

The point is that we should tell our anxious children there is not necessarily more evil in the world than there was before. It's just more available for examination, although undoubtedly that in itself might be a reason why some very sick people are committing it more publicly than in prior circumstances.

But meanwhile we should tell our kids that most people don't kill other people. There are, indeed, portentous images that create the strong impression that every street in America is under cross fire and that every shopping center, schoolhouse, and post office is in a state of siege. For the love of our children, we cannot succumb to a sense of doom or resignation because this only fosters the growing distress of our young people. We should not exacerbate their feelings of insecurity, even while taking common-sense steps to ensure their security.

I remember a situation several years ago when a youngster came to see me about his fears. "I honestly don't feel safe in this world," he told me. It was some time before the current, highly focused discussion on American violence. It was before gun buybacks, before the proliferation of gangs and gangsta rap. It should be noted that the young man, Kenneth, did not even live in the United States. At the time, I was serving a congregation in Toronto, Canada—supposedly a much safer place than any American city!

But there was still plenty to think about in terms of people harming each other. I remember that Kenneth was upset about the incidents of airline hijackings occurring at that particular time. He lamented the number of innocent people being shot down in airports from London to Paris to Munich because of terrorist activity that had nothing to do with the vast majority of its victims. "Why do people kill each other?" asked this very genuine boy who was not quite sixteen at the time.

Kenneth was surely thinking of how people kill each

other using high-caliber weapons; that is the normal context of our apprehension about this question. Kenneth's own death a few months later, at the hands of a drunk driver, made his query echo with a certain, terrible poignancy. A point can be made here for concerned youngsters who are certain that murder only happens in the style of television's police melodramas: Drinking kills, drugs kill, AIDS kills, guns kill. When a youngster asks, "Why do people kill each other?" we ought to mention that "people" includes a big circle of responsibility. Anybody who was ever human has the capacity to harm somebody else; we continue to count on the notion that most people are able to harness their evil tendencies.

The truth is that if there were no evil in the world, there would be no people, either. Some religions teach that evil is its own force, and that it even has its own satanic host who enters people's lives with bad suggestions, unsavory inclinations, and terrible temptations. I have no quarrel with anybody's religious beliefs, but I do believe that kids are scared enough as it is from what they see in the real world. They do not need the additional burden of a supernatural element that is wholly negative. We can't pretend that evil isn't a part of human life, so why pretend at all?

Teenagers will have a little bit of an easier time with evil if we tell them that evil is endemic to the human condition. "The devil made that person murder his girlfriend" is good material for a sermon, but it may not be too inspirational for a youngster who is trying to sort out a frightening array of new realities pouring in from television, the bookstore, or the hallways of his school. Remember, too, that although evil was always here, it has a prolific, modern accessory for itself: Video.

There is nowhere a teenager can't "travel" to anymore, so there is no limit to his exposure to the world's warts, either. Saddam Hussein beheads somebody in Baghdad— the kid in Birmingham knows it, sees it, dreams of it. Chinese militiamen run their tanks over college students in Tiananmen Square—junior high school students cope with the images from Long Beach to Times Square. All in all, what is being seen and heard is sometimes bad, sometimes better, always human. Evil, we need to alert our children, comes from the same place as brain tissue, heart membranes, and blood plasma.

And so does the fear that springs up through every child from time to time in this era of much trouble and even more information. My daughter, Sari, had no direct reason to do what virtually every child does sooner or later—wake up, terror-stricken, in the middle of the night. When she came running into our bedroom crying and screaming, it wasn't because anybody had actually threatened her with a pistol, a knife, or with their own body. But as she lay her head on my wife's chest, sobbing with despair, and as we both stroked her matted hair and wished that the morning would come soon, we knew in advance what she finally told us though broken gasps: "I'm afraid somebody is going to kidnap me and hurt me. I'm afraid somebody is going to shoot me with a gun."

How do you respond to a child in this situation? You look directly at her so that she can see the most important thing in the world: Your face. You listen to her as she pours out her emotions. Let the poison drain out. You put your arms around her and let her stay by you as long as she needs, because very adult-like fears have turned this teen-ager back into a child tonight. You comfort her with the knowledge that the light of morning will most assuredly come, and you explain to her that her knowledge of evil guarantees that she will know how to choose what is good.

In the morning, review your rules about malls, cars, hours, people. Your child will be listening. Remind your child that life is with people, and the fact is that some people are better than others.

CHAPTER 6

Why Is There So Much
Racism Around?

You may be surprised to learn that the above question was asked by a sixteen-year-old white girl and was directed at her black classmates. We usually assume that a question of racism has to do with negative behavior on the part of Caucasian people towards other races. We assume a lot of things. The 1990s have provided us with plenty of information about the inability of ethnic groups to honor, let alone venerate, one another. The decade has also helped every ethnic group that is honest come to terms with its own social flaws.

For years, Jewish parents were fairly certain that they could assure their children of the basic decency and fairness of virtually all Jews. Not even the constant controversy of Israel's relationship with the Palestinians was able to really call the national Jewish morality into question. Besides, while the conglomerate of the United Nations, some elements of the media, and some real terrorists combined to revile and hurt Israel, the Jewish state was quietly gathering in countless exiles, raising crops and children in the desert while rescuing hostages and victims from a number of remote and dangerous situations. Judaism seemed fairly safe from criticism.

But then a quite controversial rabbi named Meir Kahane appeared. In the 1980s, he gathered notoriety, fed his ego, and called for the removal or extermination of Arabs from the West Bank. The rabbi built a bloc of fanatical support, mainly in parts of New York and in some sections of Israel. His hateful movement transferred a lot of sympathetic fundamentalist Jews to Israel, creating havoc, murder, and terrible distrust. Kahane was gunned down in New York, but his legacy prospered in the form of a venomously separatist community that preferred to eliminate the indigenous Arabs from the biblical hills that lie between Jerusalem and the Jordan River.

When an emigrant American doctor massacred twenty-nine Muslims praying in their mosque near Hebron in early 1994, a lot of Jews all over the world realized once and for all that even Jews can be racist, crazy, or both. Tragically, the extremist Arab side more than answered the incident with a series of killings over the ensuing few weeks. Nonetheless, Jewish people, still coping emotionally and spiritually with what the Nazis did fifty years ago, were not left to think of themselves strictly as the victims in an open and volatile world.

In high school during the 1960s many of us endured the sit-ins, the disruptions, and the riots that reflected the overall agitation of the nation's cities at that time. A number of college campuses were downright perilous. We understood that America's racism was being turned over in very public and agonizing exercises of self-examination and some renewal. People, some quite famous, more quite dedicated, died in the streets. We were frightened and wary, but we also thought that we had eventually accomplished something.

I'm not quite certain why, a generation later, there is still so much racial unrest in this country. The Los Angeles riot of 1992 took more lives than any such explosion of the 1960s; the adulation of a preacher named Martin King gave way to the exploitation of a motorist named Rodney King. When we had community trouble, it was usually matched by an equal blast of idealism. Vietnam was leavened by Woodstock. No such elixir in the MTV culture: When society has trouble today, it is usually matched by yet another blast of cynicism. So while I'm not sure what exactly happened, I am very sure that teenagers today are deeply distressed by the level of racism they endure from day to day.

My younger daughter, Debra, was not quite eleven years old when she brought home her distress about her African-American classmate who wanted to know why the Jews were slave traders. This happened in 1994, thirty years after President Lyndon Johnson, a Texan, stood in the halls of Congress proclaiming that "we shall overcome." The worst impulses of the human spirit, likely delivered by ignorant parents who like some kids but who obviously hate most children, had been transposed into the culture of a fifth grade classroom in Ohio. Did this represent the attitudes of all the black children in that classroom? Obviously not. Is it dangerous nonetheless? Without question. Whatever progress we make in this troubled and violent country among social groups will be completely undone as long as parents send scornful messages via their children. We teach our children how to eat, how to dress, how to love, and we most assuredly teach them how to hate.

And it is not parents alone who influence young people in this category. Every one of us who teaches, counsels, protects or coaches others has some responsibility for what the Jewish tradition calls "repairing the world." When a role model fails, the world is a little bit broken.

Several years ago, I had the experience of being a regular visitor to the dugout of the Cleveland Indians baseball club. I was interested in learning how young men of various ethnic backgrounds work together in the atmosphere of major league sports. The team was not very good in those days, and I wondered how the manager of this club would handle the challenge.

Unfortunately, the manager of this forlorn baseball team did not inspire a lot of goodwill. The players often blamed their poor play on the condition of the old playing field, the lack of daring trades made by the front office, and the overbearing presence in their division of such heavyweights as the New York Yankees and the Toronto Blue Jays. All of these were undoubtedly factors in the perennial dismay of those years in Cleveland. But I didn't think that the prejudice in the dugout was much help, either.

As with most major league clubs, the Indians were an amalgam of players—white, black, Latin, Asian. The manager evidently preferred his players from such places as the

Dominican Republic and Cuba because he spoke to them almost exclusively. And he spoke to these players continuously in Spanish—even if English-speaking players were present or close by. There was rarely any translation or inclusiveness; Spanish was used less for instruction in these instances as it was used for a wall. There was a tawdriness about the whole thing that served to exacerbate the feelings of division among a team of once-idealistic athletes who were losing a lot more than ball games.

When I was in college, I sang with the men's glee club. In my senior year, the club crossed the Ohio River from Cincinnati for a grand tour of the South. Our destination was New Orleans; in between lay a series of performances in auditoriums and church halls from Kentucky to Mississippi. It was 1974, but—as we baritones and tenors were soon to learn—it might as well have been 1934 in such towns as Welch, West Virginia and Veramayne, Tennessee.

Arriving one afternoon in the latter community, we were greeted by the local church leaders. It was in their house of worship that we would perform our nightly repertory of show tunes, ballads, and folk songs. Our conductor, Bill Ermey, was always first off the bus. Bill, thin as a reed but endowed with an iron will that kept our libidos at bay even as our voices were in sync, would make the preliminary arrangements as to set up, equipment checks, and housing.

In this Tennessee borough, however, Bill ran into a little bit of a problem. The town fathers and mothers had peered into the windows of our charter bus and, alas, noticed a sprinkling of black faces among us fifty young men.

There would apparently be no houses available for the "Negro boys" to lodge in.

I remember Bill's face as he dragged himself up the steps of the bus. The late afternoon sun emphasized his paleness and pain. "They won't let us *all* sleep in their homes," he whispered in agony over the static-filled microphone. "Our black members are supposed to spend the night in the motel down the road."

"And they expect us to think of their church as a house of God!" I called out from near the rear, evidently already contemplating a career in the clergy. But my sentiment was being echoed in the throats and hearts of every one us who sat, stunned, in a Greyhound bus that now was the vehicle of a new and dreadful awareness.

"Well, boys," said Bill, with a wan and knowing smile, "I'm your leader. And I say that if we can't all sleep in their houses, then none of us can sing in their church."

A burst of cheering and applause rocked the bus. Bill Ermey turned his narrow back around in the doorway, leaned out, and yelled to the nearby cluster of church leaders:

"We're sorry, people, but we will not be singing here tonight. But we do propose that you have a meeting tonight in your church and ask God why these nice boys lost their voices while passing through this town of yours."

The University of Cincinnati men's glee club wound up sleeping aboard the Greyhound that night, parked alongside US 231 in a rather dreary roadside stop that sucked in the darkness. We, however, laughed and sang and eventually slept as cheerfully as our teacher's convictions had been inspired back down the road at a church with no god.

Sometimes, however, it is the children who instruct the adults. When, in early 1994, I helped chaperone a group of three hundred eighth graders to view the landmark motion picture *Schindler's List*, I was among a small group of professionals who saw and heard the enmity nibbling away between cultural groups. We also came to understand how our own naïveté can contribute towards making a bad situation worse.

Schindler's List brought a great deal home for many people. Many youngsters had never really been exposed, in this vivid fashion, to the absolute and abject horrors of the Nazi Holocaust. The Jewish community, for some time ambivalent about how to handle the burden of our own knowledge of what had happened just fifty years ago, found in this movie a painfully cathartic expression of our terror, rage, and guilt.

Revisionism about the Holocaust was already a limited but unsettling reality by the time Steven Spielberg fulfilled his creative promise to himself and his people by making this movie. I remember just a few weeks after *Schindler's List* had become generally known and widely seen, hearing Abraham Foxman, the national director of the Anti-Defamation League, tell a group of Jewish leaders who were meeting in Washington, D.C. that "these people who now claim, through supposed scholarly research and theories, that the Holocaust never happened—what they are doing is killing all the victims a second time. First they were killed physically, now they are being killed again, spiritually."

Earlier that same day in Washington, a prominent leader of the Nation of Islam had stood on the steps of the United

States Holocaust Museum and denounced the Jewish people for their "Holocaust hoax." Like some other African-American leaders of the 1990s, this individual mocked Jewish suffering and claimed that blacks had endured a much larger martyrdom in terms of scope and numbers. When kids ask me about why there is so much racism, I wonder about grownups who spend time actually engaged in counting and comparing the tragic marbles of human savagery.

When *Schindler's List* came along, a lot of us thought that its compelling realism could help kids understand the implications of human bestiality. At my daughter Sari's racially mixed school, a field trip was planned and organized. Sari and a few of her friends who had already seen the movie got up and explained its impact upon them at an assembly the day before the actual outing. A Baptist minister who is my friend and neighbor appealed directly to the African-American children: "Don't look at this movie as just a Jewish movie. Look at it and understand what people do to each other when cruelty is acceptable. It's the story of any people who suffer at the hands of others."

Most of the three hundred youngsters were transfixed the next day. A few, however, were unable to sit and view the movie with respect; it was painful for me to behold this. Some of these disrupting kids would taunt my daughter and her friends the next day about having to go see "that Jew-movie." When asked by the Jewish kids about the reverend who told them to regard the ultimate message of this powerful movie, some of them replied: "What the reverend says doesn't mean anything." Clearly, seeds of contempt had been planted in the fertile minds of some children long before a few of us thought that a motion picture could suddenly plow over the darkest gardens of the human spirit.

But the school in question did pursue the matter. Discussion groups drew the youngsters into thoughtful confrontation. Adults realized that we had been presumptuous in some ways: All four of the presenters at the initial assembly were Jewish. Wouldn't the perspective of at least one black eighth grader who previewed the movie have helped the situation? Does every young person living in this era of disposable information and saturating media violence necessarily even know that there was a Holocaust? Shouldn't the reverend and I have spoken to the kids just *after* the outing, and not just before?

As awareness of this botched and unsuccessful field trip developed, the Jewish community became outraged. Solemn conclusions about the complete social bankruptcy of the black community were weighed privately as well as publicly. Nonetheless, the youngsters at Sari's school kept on talking. They eventually moved on to other subjects, such as smoking, drugs, and teenage sex. They discovered a lot of common anxieties and concerns. The kids politely declined my offer, and that of the good reverend, to come back into the school and talk some more.

Some of the wounds from the *Schindler's List* expedition are not going to disappear. But left to their own wits, most youngsters will find their way to a reasonable amount of common ground. They are more afraid of racism than they are solicitous of it, maybe because they just know that they will eventually encounter it, in a baseball dugout, across a movie screen, or even from the pulpit of a house of God.

We should have been answering this question long before they were even old enough to start asking it.

Meanwhile, the question hangs over us like a rain cloud, because we know that any answer might very well betray more than we wish about ourselves. Why is there so much racism around? The answer has a lot to do with the fact that many of us, plain and simple, are racists.

I think that one reason for all the ethnic tension in the 1990s is that we have all tried too hard to put forward something ennobling about our individual groups. Some of it is well-meaning for ourselves while some of it is demeaning towards others. "Ethnic differences" seem to mean more than my term of preference: *Ethnic qualities*. Somehow, no cultural group seems able to feel good about itself just by expressing an enlightened self-image. It's almost as if somebody else has to be less in order for me to be more.

A key way to fight racism is promoting a sound feeling about one's own ethnic group that is based upon a genuine knowledge of its history, customs, and values. When a parent takes this approach, he or she is not likely to rely upon the denigration of one group in order to exalt the other. I tell Jews that a good response to anti-Semitism is to turn to acts of "pro-Semitism." Learning one's own heritage, becoming literate in the identifying rituals and habits of that heritage, raises the level of the discussion about culture and race. Generally speaking, members of an ethnic group who "know themselves" and exude prideful feelings based on positive impulses cannot be undone by those who come with the negative. If every group had this kind of integrity, then America could truly regard itself as a "salad" of cultures, with every element bringing something savory for the overall flavor of our national experience. It starts at home: Tell your child something good about who you are, as opposed to something bad about who somebody else is.

We cannot wait for national leadership on this. It is not forthcoming from the media, from sports figures, or from politicians. Our young people are anxious about this; bringing hatred home from school is troubling and debilitating for them.

We have to capture and create moments that will be defining for our children—just as Bill Ermey once did and the manager of the Cleveland Indians did not. We have to recognize that young people are keenly impressionable. As long as there have been parents, children have been the clay that we have molded, from Berlin to Cape Town, to Sarajevo to Los Angeles, and back to inside your own home.

CHAPTER 7

Why Do I Sometimes Feel
Like I Want to Die?

When kids become teenagers, they begin to think a lot about death and dying. One of the best things we can do to help them with this is to make sure they understand that death is final. We want to comfort them when they start to fear the prospect of death, but we also need to understand that kids *need* to fear death just a little. What we don't want to do is to mimic the habits of today's society that make death appear benign or even attractive to impressionable young men and women. The Elvis syndrome of perpetual resurrection is dangerous and irresponsible.

When celebrities live on past their deaths or suicides, then how they died and the very fact of their mortality are lost upon our emerging children. I want young people to be frightened of the way Elvis Presley or Kurt Cobain expired; instead the video and profit culture encourages a kind of national séance with Elvis. "Sightings" are reported from hamburger joints, radio stations, and mini-malls. But if Elvis lives, or if John Lennon's image can be reincarnated by electronic magic on a new Beatles compact disc, then maybe these two victims—one of self-abuse, the other of murder—aren't really dead. The message this sends to vulnerable young people is that death is not necessarily final and that fatal practices do not necessarily cause a penalty.

"In the world of posthumous fame," the *New York Times* recently stated, "a celebrity's death need not impinge on his or her marketability."

I am worried about all of this because I know that most teenagers have enough of a hard time with their awareness of mortality. Making it seem as though death is not final may bring in profits for entertainment lawyers, estate experts, and copyright specialists. It is not so profitable for young people who understand very little about royalties but a lot about night terror, and who are coping with helpless, even suicidal, feelings.

Most adolescents carry or express the feeling, from time to time, of wanting to die. On one level this is an outgrowth of realizing, for the first time, that death is real and inevitable. Sometime in early adolescence, a person is suddenly filled with the quiet dread: I am going to die someday! A particularly tender and simple layer of childhood is ripped away. Most every parent can remember, more or less, when this happened to him or her.

One of the ironies for me, as a spiritual leader, is the role that religion sometimes plays in this personal drama. It is not always a helpful role. There is a great deal of interest in death that can be found in much of organized religion. Some theological leaders point to death regularly, making it a lightning rod for their expressed persuasions. Death is a punishment, or a reward—or both. Martyrdom is ingrained into much of Scripture. A lot of bad folks die, but as many good folks die in supposedly enlightening moral scenarios. Death is not infrequently the noble conclusion; for one great Western religion, the death of its beacon hero is the magnificent crucible that started civilization all over again.

Again, I have no quarrel with anybody's religious faith, and I certainly believe deeply in what a healthy spirituality can bring to anybody at any time. But I do have a quarrel with any situation that might exacerbate a youngster's already complicated relationship with the idea of death. Nothing as profound as one's creed nor as frivolous as freeze-dried "Elvis sweat" should endanger the welfare of your child and mine by making death in any way attractive. Teenagers are already coping with intermittent bouts of death-wishing. Making them think about dying more than they have to is truly perilous.

We have already heard much over the past few years about what can be called the emotional inflation of death that is a part of our society. It may have begun with the introduction (for purely economic reasons) by the postal service of a stamp commemorating the apparently undead Elvis Presley. Glorifying a fine singer and composer who nonetheless killed himself with drugs and alcohol leaves much to be desired. The same federal government that is worried about how much cholesterol goes into a potato chip might have considered how much distortion goes into the mind of a child who, with the lick of a postage stamp, seals his already fragile relationship with mortality into an endless joke about Elvis sightings at the nearby 7-Eleven.

The transformation of death into kitsch may have started with Elvis, but it certainly continued with the very tragic Kurt Cobain. Analysts made much of the implications of Cobain's suicide; some even considered the rock singer's short and twisted life with a measure of sympathy and insight. Some very responsible parents and teachers—who knew very little about Cobain's music but who care a lot about kids—tried to turn this much-publicized suicide into an opportunity for discussing the value of human life. But the very regrettable impulse of our profit- and image-obsessed civilization to turn the ugly conclusion of a young man's life into a question of consumer viability was unimpaired. A management consultant was quoted as saying, after Kurt Cobain killed himself: "I definitely think he's going to have legs. . . . As a media move it was great."

What kind of community are we? Don't we have enough respect for our own fears not to "give legs" to the rising suspicion of young, impressionable people that death is not actually final? Is life a television soap opera where people who have been murdered or who die (still looking rosy) from terrible illnesses can nevertheless return with refurbished contracts and renewed plotlines? Or isn't life —real life—the place where, according to the Children's Defense Fund, 1 in 6 young people between the ages of 10 and 17 actually has seen or knows someone who has been shot?

Elvis may be swiveling his hips at the local launderette and Steve McQueen may have become a T-shirt riding a motorcycle, but the fact is that in the United States, children under eighteen (says the FBI) are 244% more likely to be killed by guns now than they were in 1986. None of these kids is going to ever reappear to wipe their parents' tears away or even turn over the Marvin Gaye or Bob Marley cassettes playing on the stereo.

Why do teenagers sometimes feel like dying? One reason is that society no longer treats death with the respect it deserves. It seems that some record moguls, some magazine editors, and even some preachers, have forgotten what their own trembling was like when, at the age of twelve or thirteen, they suddenly realized that life will end someday and that the end of the discussion is nothing but the grave. So, again, parents who brought our children into mortal being must consider our responsibilities to their struggle with mortality.

The impact of commercialism notwithstanding, I think that one reason that children sometimes feel like dying is that we put too much pressure on them. A good report card is a worthy goal, but is it really more worthy than your child's own feelings of worth? Our kids are constantly competing—with their classmates, with standards of fashion, with very intense social mores. The toughest thing for a youngster to compete with is himself. If he is truly able to achieve a *B* on his report card, just how much good are we accomplishing by lambasting him to get an *A*? Noting again how our celluloid civilization has already made death a benign, even glamorous option (possibly "giving legs" to some people who have chosen it), are we perhaps risking our child's safety by pushing her to be someone other than she is?

Now, most parents are not driving their kids to be such

overachievers that the kids are going to kill themselves. But suicidal feelings are a part of adolescence. Pushing a child's buttons at the wrong time must be considered treacherous. What we have to acknowledge is that every teenager ruminates about death from time to time. Rather than laying guilt upon your kid about the need for her to do well in high school because you won't have enough money to send her to college unless she pulls in scholarship money; rather than incessantly chiding your youngster for being too heavy and therefore causing you embarrassment; rather than destroying your teenager's self-esteem by *ever* telling him that he's a disappointment (the feeling might be mutual); rather than all of this, it might be better to look, listen, and love.

All of the above situations are important, requiring frank and generous conversation with the child you brought into this world. College funds, one's weight and health, the manner in which parents and children regard each other, are all normal sources of tension and evaluation in a family. Most young people today, who are already exposed to more than just this litany of emotional and social pressures in school and elsewhere—and who generally know much more than we give them credit for—are perfectly able to discuss these matters with a caring parent. A teenager does have a responsibility, for example, to do his best in school in order to achieve academic and fiscal goals related to college. But he is not responsible to loathe himself in any way because of the financial predicament of his parents, or because he really does just get average grades in a world that pushes almost everybody.

Everybody needs to calm down just a bit. Kids have always contemplated suicide; today the world is one big video manual showing you how to do it. Better than criticizing your child too much, you ought to listen for signs of self-hate. Moodiness, angry eruptions, evasiveness, brazenness—all could mean something serious. An obsession with someone, especially someone dead, is deserving of your attention. But nobody is more deserving of your attention than your own child who—because he's a kid struggling with mortality—is going to consider death from time to time. Indeed, a parent must monitor a child at all times, and, when things get really hectic or confusing, absolutely call for the intervention of a good psychiatric professional. Don't stand on ceremony!

When fourteen-year-old Jenna swallowed an entire bottle of Tylenol several years ago, severely poisoning her liver, I went to her bedside and prayed. Miraculously, she survived. When I was finally able to ask her why she did this to herself, I wasn't surprised by the answer: "I can't do enough things well."

Here was a child who was a gourmet cook, a brilliant flutist, and an accomplished gymnast. Her parents, who had announced their divorce just prior to Jenna's suicide attempt, are also exceptionally talented and brilliant people. But they had forgotten to do one thing: Listen to their only child. A lot had been achieved in that home, except the one thing that is most important.

I have attended to a number of other situations like this over the years that did not end like Jenna's. Sometimes, the self-inflicted gunshot wound, the hanging rope or the bottle of pills were preceded by too much other poison. The liver may have survived one time; the heart usually does not.

It is a fact that teenagers, in the normal course of events, consider death. This is a delicate rite of passage. Meanwhile, this society is already forgiving or exalting the idea of death. You may have inadvertently driven your child to suicidal feelings. Go find your child and give him or her some tenderness.

CHAPTER 8

When I Die, Will Anybody Remember Me?

Inside a simple apartment, within a nondescript high-rise building, above an indifferent freeway, and overlooking a yawning shopping complex there lies a shrine. A mother has sought out the corners of this modest residence and solemnly laid down photographs, medallions, clippings, and tributes. Candles are lit in some places as the visitor comes to pay a call. A mother remembers her daughter in a small dwelling given over to the processes of memory and healing.

The daughter was a remarkable woman with many talents. Her stunning physical beauty only added to the luster of her presence. Thick, coal-black hair hung over a graceful and intelligent face that peers out at the visitor from the photographs and articles. The departed woman, Judith Resnik, was not just a famous astronaut. She was a physicist, an academician and—for good measure—a concert pianist. She did not plan to die the day she boarded the space shuttle *Challenger* with six of her colleagues who also perished in the sky. Few people plan or know of their deaths. We spend most of our time trying to live.

I was in this sad apartment because Judith Resnik's mother had phoned me. She saw an article I had just written in the local newspaper that noted the seventh anniversary of the *Challenger* disaster. Over the phone, she thanked me for helping to keep her daughter's memory alive. Since she lives in our community, it was appropriate for my wife Cathy and I to subsequently pay a call upon the mother of a woman I have truly admired and whose memory is an inspiration for many young people.

Sarah, the mother, showed us pictures of Judy, and told us of her daughter's great ambitions. The experience was particularly meaningful because it refocused the idea of Judy Resnik's death from a national headline to a personal agony. The television coverage, the global convocation, the presidential eulogy—all passed from the scene as Cathy and I heard the direct anguish and the private tribute spoken to us around a coffee table by a mother who will never forget her child.

Sarah will eventually pass on herself, and some stranger will most likely come and box up the apartment that serves as a kind of mausoleum for Judy Resnik. Sarah is not blessed with warm and extended family connections; she grieves for her famous daughter mainly by herself. But Cathy and I will always be changed by our visit that day, and our recollections of it—and of Judy's life—will continue. When somebody dies, others remember—especially if people are willing to listen and learn from the stories of other lives.

I often think about Sarah and her daughter when somebody asks me about living, dying, and being remembered. Of course, not everybody was as eminent as Judith Resnik, nor do most people die such tragic and public deaths. But it is not Judy's fame that is the point. People do not just remember her because she was an astronaut. What makes Judy memorable is the fact that she lived up to her every potential. That is possible, and maybe even required of every one of us who wants to live life fully and therefore be remembered.

When a teenager asks about the point of existence as against the reality of mortality, he or she may just be trying to ascribe some greater meaning to the experience of living. The first thing to do when confronted by this question is to sort it out: Are you asking because you are feeling depressed? Do you have any doubts that you want to live? In keeping with the discussion of chapter seven, we must be certain that a youngster is not asking this kind of question because of a specific emotional problem, but because of a general philosophical inquiry into the value and meaning of life. That kind of inquiry is healthy, normal, and a good springboard for a talk about the greatest gift there is—life itself.

It must be made clear that as long as people are willing and able to talk to each other, nobody is ever forgotten! Grandparents who were once there, a cousin who helped encourage and define life, a friend who brought light and promise to us—all inform our lives each and every time members of a family share feelings and values. In fact, one of the most important reasons we are created in families is so that no one is ever forgotten. And every person who ever lived has had the potential to touch, teach, and even inspire somebody else. It's not fame that guarantees immortality; it's the ability to love and be loved. I particularly realized that the day Judy Resnik's mother cried her tears in my presence. Suddenly, the glossy photograph of Judy in the magazine Sarah was holding at that moment was just not as important as the pages in her heart that we were turning together.

I remember coming "home" recently to Cincinnati, where I was raised, and attending the Passover seder in my mother's house. Moments like this, at Passover, at Christmas, at any time when a family gathers in several generations, are not just passages through this life. They are the times when we realize just how much tenderness for each other can be released just by remembering people.

As we gathered around the holiday table that Passover, my younger brother handed me a copy of the Haggadah that had clearly been used before. The Haggadah is the service book used at the seder; it follows a prescribed order of prayers, songs, and blessings that combine to remind us of the great freedom saga of Egypt and Israel. We literally eat, drink, sing, and smell the story. We all follow along in the book, passing through not only the history of a people, but also the personal histories that keep a family alive.

For my brother and my sister and me, the seder has a certain poignancy. Our father always led the elaborate ceremony. We can't help but miss him very much when the holiday table is set and one of us now has the responsibility of leadership. We look at our own young children around the shiny table and understand that they will grow up one day and remember when we led the seder. If we are good parents now, they will miss us then, but we will also have inspired them to continue being a family that knows how to celebrate special moments. It will not be a question of how well-known we were. It will be a question of how well-loved.

I realized, on that particular seder night, that the Haggadah passed to me was very special indeed. It was the one my father had used each and every Passover night. His notes and commentary were inscribed along the margins and in between the paragraphs. I felt such a rush of nostalgia and connection as I recognized his very meticulous handwriting, his fussy directions. It was as if he were still there among us! Enough time has passed since his death that we could even chuckle affectionately at his documented management of a family dinner, but the underlying and bittersweet reality was that my father will not be forgotten.

Nor, as it turned out, will his ability to lead us vanish from our midst. At one point in the seder, which my brother was conducting that evening, we were a bit uncertain as to what page should come next. The Haggadah is long and complicated; aside from the major and key passages, not every family follows it in precisely the same fashion. It is permissible to skip over some of the added texts, or to select some prayers more meaningful at a given time. "Where should we turn next?" my brother mused out loud.

I looked down at the page in front of me. My father's handwritten answer jumped out at me: "Here, turn to page twenty-seven, and ask the children to sing." I looked up again and spoke to the table: "He has the answer for us in the book." I informed the family of the instruction and everyone promptly turned to page twenty-seven. Soon the children sang the song on that page and the adults joined in, satisfied and comforted that, even though people eventually die, they need not be forgotten. No one is ever lost to us completely as long as we are willing to look for the notes they have left for us in the margins of our lives.

We need to encourage our children to focus on the handwriting of their lives. If a teenager is creative, and if he or she is encouraged to fulfill as much as is reasonable and possible, that teenager will not likely feel that the end of life implies the end of memory. I have always treasured the old rabbinic notion that "God created the world, but people are creating it." An astronaut's cherished medal, a grandmother's special recipe for pie, a father's scrawled notes in a book of celebration—all add up to the equation that if we leave something behind, people will remember us.

Whenever I perform a wedding ceremony, I require that the bride and groom bring something of themselves to the occasion. Regardless of the family circumstance, we all come from other people. This realization realigns the focus on life rather than the end of life. I ask the bride to bring a set of candlesticks that were used by her mother, or a grandmother, or anyone special whose memory sheds light on the milestone. I ask the groom, in turn, to bring a kiddush cup—a wine goblet that has also passed through the generations. We use these important and very holy objects in the ceremony; acquiring them gently forces a family to reflect upon old hands, remembered songs; departed voices that nonetheless still speak to us.

Tell your teenager about his or her ancestors. When a youngster feels he is really part of a continuing family story, he will not be so worried about fading memories. Not long ago, I found out that my grandfather, who had the exact same name as me, was a butcher. I had no idea! His tombstone in a humid valley of central Israel just carries our common name. I never really knew much about him until I asked my aunt while visiting the family in Tel Aviv.

My grandfather was a butcher. Sarah's daughter was an astronaut. What will your children one day say that you were? What will you leave behind so that as little as possible will be forgotten about what you feel in your heart right now? Let your kid know today.

CHAPTER 9

When Will the World End?

When young people ask this question, they are generally referring to two categories: The end of the world from natural causes and the end of the world caused by the unnatural behavior of people towards each other. The violence of nations concerns kids, but they also wonder a great deal about the fragility of our environment, our natural resources, our sun and stars.

Not too long ago, a comet named Shoemaker-Levy 9 crashed into the planet Jupiter. The mountain-sized chunks of space refuse caused a fair amount of damage to the large planet; some scientists compared the impacts to nuclear explosions. A lot of us here on earth were intrigued enough to follow this galactic event in the media; it drew us in because it was big, beyond our control, and even a bit frightening.

The planet Jupiter is massive and indifferent. It is a swirling, striped, red conglomerate of poisonous gasses, fire, and rock. Nobody lives there. Nonetheless, the reality of such a spinning globe being shaken by missile meteors was enough to send some people thinking: When will the world end?

It was not the comet, however, that prompted one teenager to ask me the question. She was thinking about it long before anybody had ever heard of two scientists named Shoemaker and Levy. There is enough uncertainty in the world of any teenager to make her wonder about the fragility—if not the mortality—of the world in which we all dwell.

From a global point of view, almost every youngster wonders about the end of the world. I recall the relief of having it explained to me over twenty-five years ago. A special exhibit at the local museum of natural history referred to the eventual disintegration of the sun. "Not to worry," we were told. The sun would continue in its present state for quite a few millennia. I felt badly for whoever was going to be around at that time, but generally removed the whole problem from my stream of consciousness.

Later, however, came the issues of ozone depletion, marine contamination, and global warming. There is no question, for example, that teenagers today do not have the carefree access to sunbathing and tanning that we did a generation ago. The sun is not exactly the same hot friend that it was a few years ago. Parents are legitimately concerned about skin cancer; going to the beach or just to the athletic field involves a fair amount of planning and sunscreen ointments. Evidence suggests that there is a hole in the sky that lets in dangerous, unfiltered rays. I know that my daughters leave behind the traditional tanning lotions when they go out in the sun and that they carry ointments that protect them *from* sunlight. This strikes me as being both prudent and somewhat sad.

It's a far cry from the extremes we used to employ in order to get darker from the sun: Remember the combination of iodine and baby oil? That was the tanning equivalent of smoking unfiltered cigarettes; the effect was direct and intense. Well, no youngster—and no adult—should smoke cigarettes, but one could argue that life was a bit more fun when you didn't have to think about a melanoma when planning for the beach or the pool.

I suppose it's understandable, given all the changes in science and technology, and the reports of solar shifts, threatened species, earthquakes, and new viruses, for some to wonder if the world is on some kind of brink. We must give our youngsters some helpful and hopeful perspective.

The truth is that the world is not ending. Some extra sunscreen and an undisciplined media screaming ominous figures at us do not add up to doomsday. In some ways, the world is just beginning, and I want every youngster to realize that a great deal of good is unfolding in a world bursting with information, knowledge, and not a little bit of promise.

When a teenager expresses fear for the welfare of the planet, it is important to consider a few things with him or her. Science has yielded us a number of positive and encouraging developments that point to an improving situation for the world and its inhabitants. One example is life expectancy—not just in quantity but also in quality.

Many diseases that inhabited our world and affected our outlooks on life have been essentially eradicated. Yes, there is a disconcerting reemergence of tuberculosis, and the HIV virus—as we well know—is a specific and frightful presence in today's civilization. Yet people are still living longer and generally healthier lives. More teenagers than ever have living and vital grandparents. Society as a whole is not yet fully addressing the delicate and urgent issues of geriatric life, nor do we have enough respect for the collective wisdom and value of our increasingly aging population. But the fact remains that a teenager today, with good personal care and a measure of luck, can really expect to live to a ripe old age.

Statistically, cancer is no longer the pervasive killer that it once was. One misconception about this disease is that, as some people say, "It seems to be everywhere—more than ever before." It's not true! What is everywhere is the diagnostic ability to isolate and quite often treat lymphomas, sarcomas, and other such ailments in people of every age. Young people, unfortunately, have always died of cancer. We hear more often about this kind of tragedy these days because we hear more often about *everything* going on in civilization. There was every kind of difficulty affecting and even ending human lives long before we developed the ability to broadcast virtually every drama occurring in the shrinking "world house."

Not so long ago, young fathers died more often of sudden heart attacks. Sadly enough, today's general stress load, plus the economic pressures (and real opportunities) that put more women in the workforce have also placed a new cardiac toll on the mothers and daughters of our society.

But the fact is that heart disease has decreased dramatically over the past several years. People are getting second and third chances because of increasingly routine bypass operations, angioplasty, and a general awareness of cardiovascular health. Nutrition, exercise, stress management are all at least serious options that people in their teens are considering for themselves and their parents. Generally speaking, even though the world seems to be a depressing and dangerous place so much of the time, and even though the health kick of recent years may be waning somewhat, we have to remind our children of the facts: People are living longer and better lives than ever before in history. Yes, beef is back to some degree, and we have to accept that American children are generally fatter than they once were. But we can't conclude that, because of the preponderance of oat bran muffins and nonfat yogurts now available at even the gasoline station minifood marts, that the country is suddenly on the road to maximum digestive and vascular health. There are more options on the grocery shelves and across food labels and in salad-bar bins. It's so easy for young people to feel a sense of doom about their bodies, their lives, their futures. We must start with some positive facts that are so often obliterated in our soap opera culture of trouble and perversion, and afternoon talk shows that thrive upon the absurd and disheartening. In spite of all the noise, the world is not ending, it's actually opening—warts, accomplishments, and all.

People often say that anything is possible. This is a virtuous attitude that is invariably useful in almost any situation, global or personal. Beyond the natural environment, teenagers worry about the environment that exists between people themselves. There will probably never be a time, as discussed in chapter five, when people will absolutely stop harming each other or stop abusing nature. But good things and stirring developments do surprise us sometimes. I was witness to just such an occurrence recently on the White House lawn.

Just a few short years ago, hardly anyone could have imagined there being peace between Jews and Arabs in the Middle East. In some ways, the trouble goes all the way back to Jacob and Esau of the Bible. It certainly has been a focused confrontation during this century. Both Jews and Arabs have lived in the land known as Palestine; a set of difficult circumstances and a tradition of hatred have made this conflict as seemingly irresolvable as it is biblical.

But I saw the famous handshake with my own eyes. It was a bright and sunny September morning in Washington when Yasir Arafat, leader of the PLO, shook hands with Yitzhak Rabin, the prime minister of Israel. I sat next to the kind congressman who had invited me to this historic occasion, and realized that we both were weeping as wild applause broke out among the several hundred dignitaries assembled that day outside the White House. This had been an unthinkable scenario just weeks earlier. We were seeing a dream played out before our very eyes.

In the Middle East, the road to peace is still very complicated, and there have been heartbreaking setbacks. But people can begin to resolve even the most difficult of problems. I think that every teenager who focuses on worldwide doom should be asked to consider the various extraordinary steps towards conflict resolution that have been taking place in the past few years. From the Middle East to South

Africa to the newly unified Germany, breathtaking events have turned back some vociferous traditions of malice and bigotry. The world is far from perfect, but the global television network that brought us the heartbreaking death marches of Rwanda has also brought a lot of people and some fresh ideas into play and discussion.

Every youngster today should hear his or her parents describe the days of the Cold War. Our generation grew up in an atmosphere of nuclear hostility, East-West alliances, and schoolhouse atomic bomb shelters. The Soviet Union was a frightening and intimidating reality in our lives. We were raised to hate and suspect everything about that civilization that was deemed an "evil empire" by a very popular president not so many years ago. We both feared and loathed the Berlin Wall to the point that its crumbling gave us a certain anxiety about losing our dependency upon its clear message. But it was a great thing that happened in Berlin and in so many other European places in the lifetimes of our teenage children. We ought to stress this to our kids because they may not understand, in between MTV and other distractions, that from the political point of view the world is actually less likely to suddenly end than it was just a little while ago. I think that every parent will do his or her child some good by telling the stories of a once-banished union leader named Walesa who became the president of Poland, the author and playwright named Havel who leads the formerly oppressed Czech Republic, and the black man named Mandela who came out of a white prison to restore and preside over South Africa.

No, the world is not ending. In some ways, it's just beginning all over again.

Meanwhile, every parent and child has a significant set of responsibilities in the category of continuing the world. Clearly, the earth is more than politics and armaments. It is also a delicate balance of water, air, and soil. Any discussion with your youngster about the possible end of the world is a good opportunity for a family to come to terms together with our inherent need to save the world.

Teenagers today, whether they realize it or not, are blessed to live in a world of recycling, litter control, and pollution standards. Industrial plants and projects no longer operate without state and federal regulations regarding their smokestacks and waste. Automobiles are subject to rather stringent emission and safety controls; we all know that these and similar efforts are imperfect and not inviolate. But they do exist, as does the prevailing mind-set among most people that throwing a piece of garbage on the ground is unacceptable, that smoking a cigarette in a public place is almost criminal, that the earth is basically a fragile place.

This whole way of looking at things is a relatively recent and welcome phenomenon. We seem to no longer take the universe for granted. A rash of natural disasters, heat waves, brutal winters, unmerciful floods, and chemical spills have awakened most good people to the earth's prevailing frailty. The washing up of contaminated hospital syringes on formerly pristine seashores a few summers ago was a shocking and revealing episode for many people. There are many grave and precarious problems that continue to face us ecologically, but the fact is that lakes and rivers are cleaner than they were, that urban air is generally more breathable, and that some previously threatened animal species (such as the bison and the American bald eagle) have made welcome comebacks because enough people decided to create legislation and attitudes that will help, in fact, to continue the world.

But there remains a great deal of work to do. When a teenager asks about the end of the world, we need to first reassure him or her about the many positive trends that do offer much hope. But we need to also ask that teenager: "What are *you* going to do to make sure the world continues?" An adolescent who lives, eats, and makes refuse in a civilization has just as much responsibility to this question as does any adult. We need to also help that youngster realize that "the world" he's asking about is much bigger than the immediate surroundings of bedroom, house, school, and local eatery.

In Canada, a nation of rigorous environmental rules, acid rain (to some degree created in American skies) continues to infect the forests and waterways of Ontario and other provinces. In western Africa, Ivory Coast peasants and timber cutters are mowing down trees at an alarming rate that threatens to simply destroy the important and nourishing wilderness of that region. A similar massacre of forests is continuing relentlessly on the Indonesian islands. In Brazil, there are endless fires that are wiping out the world's greatest rain forest.

Some people are very tired of hearing about the rain forests. But the fact is that a tropical rain forest represents the richest natural environment on the face of this planet. Apparently, the rain forests occupy just 7 percent of the world's land area. Remarkably, however, these thick and tangled forests—laden with dense humidity, countless varieties of living things, carpeted with deep and luscious canopies of vegetation and vinery—contain over half of the world's species of plants and animals. A key aspect of the world *will* come to an end if these rain forests are left to rot and die.

There are more people in the world than ever before. There is an understandable need to clear wilderness areas in order to make way for communities. But there is a crisis here that any teenager should come to understand, because it's his or her world that is being threatened in this sense. In India, loggers are wiping out the life-giving forests. In the Philippines and in Malaysia, lumber conglomerates are systematically deforesting the countryside. Miners, dairy farmers, and sugarcane growers are doing the same in sections of eastern Australia. It's happening also in places such as Bolivia, Peru, Ghana, and Nicaragua.

Yet all this represents but one element of environmental trauma that harms a very busy and tired world. I still wonder about the unimaginable damage done to the water and fish of the Persian Gulf by the terrible oil fires deliberately set several years ago by the dictator of Iraq. I worry about the beautiful wadis and graceful ospreys of the Sinai Desert that are not being cared for properly by Egypt. And, like anybody else, I am concerned about California—where an uncanny series of natural disasters and human indignities have burned, flooded, and broken one of the most graceful confluences of seawater, hills, and valleys ever designed by God.

When will the world end? One thing to consider is the earth's remarkable resiliency. It's still here, in spite of the cruelty done to it by the twentieth century alone. Between

1939 and 1945, over twenty million human beings were killed in the midst of the greatest man-made inferno ever undertaken. If the Second World War and its Holocaust and its Hiroshima did not combine to end the world, then it's hard to say what really can.

Several years ago, a series of intense brushfires almost destroyed the magnificent Yellowstone National Park of Wyoming and Montana. The park's geysers and hot springs, its evergreen forests, limestone terraces, moose, mule deer, and white pelicans were all quite threatened by this natural disaster. It was difficult for an army of rangers and fire-fighters to contain the fires; the soils of Yellowstone emerged scorched and scarred.

But the earth has its seasons. Several months later, a new layer of brightly colored vegetation began to emerge along the grounds of this great preserve. Scientists and naturalists were amazed and delighted. In short, the very ash that had accumulated from the natural remains of pines, firs, and spruce trees—and had sunk in with the burnt residue of a wide variety of wildflowers—now mixed into the sods and fertilized the earth into rebirth. The whole process of regeneration occurred in nature. Even the most hardened of scientists shook their heads in wonder.

When will the world end? Only when we stop caring about it. Only when we stop noticing that, in spite of us, it has a life of its own.

CHAPTER 10

Do Science and Religion
Go Together?

It was just outside of the village of Haliburton, Ontario, well into the thick woods one night, that I experienced a wonderful, dual revelation involving both science and religion. I had walked down the road a bit from our summer-camp lodgings, breathing in the fresh Canadian air. A fine stillness loomed in the pure night. Coming to a clearing, I looked skyward and caught my breath short. I had never seen so many stars!

Galaxies streaked across the celestial dome. Like so many noiseless fireworks, the spots and flares of astral life punctured the darkness with star fire and light. Underneath the Gemini, Pegasus, the Little Bear, and the Big Dipper I felt both awe and my own marked smallness. I searched my memory for the full cosmic map learned so long before. The astronomical explanation for this night dance eluded me, however. I realized, as a shooting star fell gracefully across the horizon, that all of this was simply God's glitter.

Before departing the magical clearing, I noticed that some of the stars, in fact, displayed varying hues. One star shone particularly blue and another gave off a reddish illumination. Like glowing wrinkles in the firmamental leather, these colored inconsistencies told me that even the sky leaves behind the fingerprints of its creator.

Touched spiritually by the heavens, I sprinted back to my cabin. Cathy slept undisturbed, but I was now affected by a delicious restlessness. Like some Taoist monk, I felt spontaneously woven into the global flow of day, night, soil, and sky. I felt a quiet intuition about the stars, and was filled with a peaceful kind of inner electricity. Acting on this soft energy, and yearning to bridge the distance between myself and anywhere else, I turned on the radio next to my bunk.

This is when the second wonder occurred. Keeping the volume low, I turned the dial carefully to the frequency of a radio station I know in Cincinnati—several hundred miles southwest of Haliburton. This AM station carries the broadcasts of the Cincinnati Reds baseball club; even though it is a "clear-channel" station, I was still amazed when the static settled and I was able to listen to the play-by-play of my hometown team. There I was, huddled in a wooden cabin in an Ontario forest, filled with celestial voltage and the correct frequency, receiving the account of the balls and strikes across the stars and suns of a very cozy nighttime sky.

The galaxies, though made of space gasses and fire, were nonetheless the suspended evidence of my spirituality. The ball game came to me via electromagnetic technology. One was religion and the other was science. I received them both comfortably; together they encouraged me on what could have been a black and lonely night far away from home. As Albert Einstein was once quoted as saying: "Religion without science is blind. Science without religion is lame."

Granted, a visit with the stars and a baseball broadcast from home do not make a definitive equation about God and the sciences. But when a youngster asks me if these two go together, I do honestly remember my little nocturnal revelation in Haliburton. And I do believe that science and religion are perfectly suited to each other, and that, in fact, they exist in harmony.

I think that a lot of this discussion has to do with the question of creation. When teenagers talk about God and science, they invariably ask about who made the world and why. They want to feel sophisticated about physics and natural law, but they also want to feel that the world was not set off spinning without a warm hand to balance it. I believe that every child and adult can be nourished by both factors when contemplating the nighttime sky, the sunlit shore, a simple flower, or the face of another human being.

It was even before the canonization of the Hebrew Scripture that men and women, gazing at scientific phenomena, wrote down creation lore that started with God. The sequence of creating that appears in the Book of Genesis is to some degree an echo of Babylonian and Egyptian sources: They all basically tell the story of firmament, dry land, luminaries, and human persons following each other into being, followed by a deity who rests and contemplates what was made. Like the Old Testament account, the Babylonian legend, called Enuma Elish, starts with water. The Egyptian stories also include primeval water, and reports of a higher power breathing life into the nostrils of man. The idea of a human being who is the image of the creator permeates all these old stories. Natural, physical elements clash, expand, meld, and diverge in all the descriptions; they all can be reasonably fitted, for example, into the famous big bang theory. But none of these traditions, all so similar, are without the tender evidence of some kind of God. In other words, the various devotions have no particular problem with the physics. It's just that God started all the physics.

Christianity asserts categorically that God created all the cosmic material out of nothing. Many pious Christians are quite endowed intellectually and philosophically; they are not conflicted by the combination of religion and science. Albert Einstein was a committed Jew who invented the theory of relativity as well as the notion that "God does not play dice." The rabbinic tradition, which grappled with much of the dilemmas and contradictions of the physical world, nevertheless asserts that God alone—and no assisting angels—willed the world into being: "With ten words was the world created."

I have often been fascinated with what the Hindus have to say. Since all of us in the human family have been trying to pinpoint evidence of God all these years, and since God seems so elusive in some ways, it is interesting to note the explanation of creation offered in the Hindu *lila*, the play of God. This myth describes the creation of the world by God's act of self-sacrifice. The world is holy because God becomes the world and the world becomes God.

Even the Greeks, who passed along their important foundation of solid science, and who basically gave us the original theory of endless matter, nevertheless asserted that the universe as a whole must have a cause. Plato and Aristotle agreed that the world as we know it is the result of a series of causes and effects. But they thought of God as being the first cause. Particles, energy, winds, rocks, quasars, and quantum leaps are all fine, scientific and discernible. But God is still the first cause, even as the rabbis of ancient Palestine wrote poetically about the "divine spark" that ignited everything else that can be proven logically.

There is a certain irony about the twentieth century. More scientific discoveries that have absolutely revolutionized human progress have been made in this century than ever before. The theory of relativity, the breakdown of the atom, the new world of quantum-field activity are all among the astonishing breakthroughs of this century. Just about everything, from the stars of Haliburton to the dinosaur bones of Wyoming, can be rationally configured by physics. Yet, as we know, the search for God has hardly ever been more intense in our society—even as some modern thinkers are finding interesting parallels between the scientific quantum theory and Oriental mysticism. In the end, there is always the unpredictable and the unexplained; in the end, as in the beginning, there is the need for a mind, a soul, a God to account for such things as the rush of rapture in a human heart, or the appearance of a bluish or reddish star amidst the otherwise white lights of heaven.

The Bible never tells us what exactly is meant by "six days of creation." There is no description of clockwork or twenty-four hour days; six days could have been six million units of time that have nothing to with the digital timer in everybody's bedroom. Therefore, evolution is entirely compatible with Genesis. Meanwhile, religion, from Zen to Islam, is basically a flight from loneliness. The Babylonians who watched the Milky Way, the Egyptians who envisioned divine nostrils, the Hebrews who chanted prayers according to the rhythm of the harvest seasons, all craved the presence of gentleness and friendship in the mystery that was bigger than all of them. All of these people, in various degrees, wrote significant astrological graphs, devised numerologies, built bridges, and charted the oceans. But none of them, even the scientific Platonists of Greece, could comprehend existence without the hand of God. They all pursued science, even as the twentieth century has mastered it in many ways. But religion is science with love.

Children are, technically, physiological organisms produced in the scientific processes of birth. But what parent regards his or her child as just an act of anatomy? We don't even think about the chemical equations of water, plasma, and bone that make up the living being who is our youngster. We look at our personal act of creation with, hopefully, love and pride and concern and interest, even as most traditions hold on to the belief that God has the same kind of regard for the whole act of creation. A child who isn't loved is like science without spirit; such a child is as lonely as physics without poetry.

In fact, this applies to the relationship between any two human beings. "Animatronics" are fine for Disney

World; people are yearning, suffering, and dreaming in the real world.

On a recent June evening, a group of nine older people climbed aboard a small elevator that serviced a suburban apartment building. They had just completed a friendly session of card playing and conversation; the host couple saw their guests to the elevator doors. The entire group, with the exception of one, my mother, had been born in Europe and were survivors of the Holocaust. My mother's husband, my stepfather, had endured six years of his adolescence in Polish and German concentration camps. But tonight, Meir was not thinking about the Nazis. He had enjoyed the cards, the fellowship, the Yiddish, the coffee, the laughter.

A few seconds later, Meir would be back in the camps. The host of the evening, Mr. Goldstein, heard the screams and the sickening sound of the crash five floors below. Mr. Goldstein ran back into his apartment and dialed 911 with shaking, sweating hands. The doors of the elevator had shut and the metal box simply fell straight down the shaft with its victims, including my mother, my stepfather, and the seven others who had already seen too much horror in their lifetimes. One woman died instantly, while all the others suffered severe and debilitating injuries that have changed the course of their remaining lives. Indeed, the husband of the woman who was first killed passed away in his hospital bed a month later.

The newspapers and the television stations in Cincinnati were quite sensitive to the fact that the elevator victims were Holocaust survivors. The local and some national media assumed, almost understandably, that my mother had also been in the camps. The fact is that my mother was born in Israel. But when she married Meir, she also married into the complicated, somewhat withdrawn world of those with memories usually too painful to even share, except among themselves—sometimes.

Both my mother and my stepfather sustained compound fractures to both legs, along with shattered heels and ankles. My mother crushed her femur, my stepfather received lacerations that were similar to burns. Both of them endured several operations and a great deal of therapy. Many in the unlucky group coped with spinal damages, amputations of limbs, and some paralysis.

My mother's courage and limited good fortune did not prevent her from experiencing serious bouts of depression in the weeks and months that followed. A group of her dearest friends had suffered this all together. There would be no more relaxed card games for this circle. For my stepfather Meir, however, there would be additional problems.

I was by no means the first person, or the only rabbi, who immediately worried about the specific terror of a former Holocaust victim being shut up in a falling box. The Nazis had done things just as horrifying to the Jews—but deliberately. Meir didn't speak about his own long ordeal very much. He is a generally upbeat man who seems to have hid away a slice of his soul.

But I did know that he had suffered terribly as a young man. His adolescence was the national equivalent of that elevator ride: He happened to board life, and have its doors shut, at the wrong place at the wrong time. In a sense, he was pushed down a Polish shaft for all six years of the Second World War.

Through all of it, Meir once told me, he swore that he would live. The sudden executions, the random pillages, the wanton and unbelievable bursts of cruelty towards babies and old people all failed to break his determination. "I'm a survivor," he said to me with sad but open eyes.

Now, fifty years after the madness, Meir lay in a Cincinnati hospital room. He had come through the initial intensive convalescence following the elevator disaster. His injuries were critical but stabilized. The problem was that Meir had been continually staring into space and was not responding to his doctors, his family, or his friends. Though not pretending to be a doctor, I wondered if the terrible trauma had sent Meir back to the camps.

At last, after a few weeks of working with him, his care team and his family were able to elicit a few words and a sense of familiarity from him. Mostly, however, Meir cried whenever someone he recognized came close. He was fairly conversant on this particular occasion when I came to visit.

His tears and his sobs were actually welcoming to me. "Pray for me!" he repeated. "The rabbis have been praying for me." I looked directly into his eyes and thought I saw Cracow.

We talked a little bit about his strength and bravery. He was doing better, I thought. He held my hand resolutely. He asked about people, especially my mother, who was recuperating in a different facility and whom he missed very much. I told him again that we were all so deeply proud of him.

ward with unmistakable stubbornness. I knew that he meant this on several levels. Then his tears came again.

"You *are* a survivor," I practically sang to him. "God has saved you again because you are a good man. Do you want to pray with me?"

"Yes, yes," he choked on his emotions. "I'll pray with you."

At last, Meir relaxed. He breathed easier. I beheld the tubes and the medical hookups that gave his thin frame nutrients, oxygen, and life. I saw his lips quiver as he began to whisper the words of his prayer again.

Science supported his body, religion carried his soul. It happens every day in a world blessed with both vigilant technology and caring spirits. God wanted to quench human thirst, and then physics combined two units of hydrogen with one of oxygen to make water. Clouds form, rain falls, human souls are drenched with both joy and grief. Meir's tubes connect him to himself while he finds a way, without a trace of science, to connect himself to creation. "The rabbis are praying for me," he says, as the intravenous tube drips one drop at a time.

Do science and religion go together? A teenager will feel much more secure about the world around him when we show him that life is the combined song of both. Why separate these two sides of the cosmic coin? Why separate anything from anything else that services the quality of this predicament we call life? We parents and professionals ought to consider how fragmented our civilization is to begin with: Race from race, poor from rich, farm from city, east from west, technology from nature, religion from science—and, alas, parent from child. We are raising our teenagers in a car pool culture that is regimented, scheduled, disparate, remote. We probably don't mean for it to be this way, but the resulting efficient, driven way of life to which we all subscribe leaves these children feeling serviced but empty.

The truth is that the world is a whole, even as creation is a total collection, from God to geometry. By not submitting to the fragmentation that starts the second your clock radio goes off in the morning and you become a running human calendar, we just might reassure our kids that we are all part of something born of the same creation. Remind your youngster that, in God's eyes, it all runs together—galaxies, radio signals, Holocausts, elevator crashes, praying lips, dripping tubes, singing hearts—from Haliburton to Cincinnati to the Milky Way to the home in which you and your children live.

Do science and religion go together? The best merging point is the very child who stands before you, and, in living and growing before your eyes, answers the question with a resounding *yes*.

CHAPTER 11

Why Is Money So Important?

In the Broadway musical and motion picture, *Fiddler on the Roof*, which is actually a compilation of stories originally penned in Yiddish by the great Jewish folk writer Sholom Aleichem, the beleaguered main character, Tevye the Milkman, attempts to arrange the marriage of his oldest daughter. It seems that the town's wealthiest Jewish citizen, Lazar Wolf the Butcher, an older widower, has his heart set on marrying the young woman. Because Tevye knows that this will ensure financial security for his daughter, he agrees to the match with a man as old as Tevye himself.

In the morning, Tevye tells his daughter "the great news." His wife, Golde, claps and shouts for joy. The daughter, Tzeitel, who is secretly in love with a young tailor much more her age, is clearly heartsick. Suddenly, she begs her father to release her from this match—an unheard-of proposition in that time and place (Russia, around 1905). After her pleading, Tevye relents, looking skyward in frustration, but nevertheless feeling his daughter's anguish.

Stroking his daughter's hair, he mutters: "I suppose it was not ordained that you should have all the comforts of life."

During this interchange, the family's current boarder, Perchik, who is a budding Bolshevik and who already has his eye on Tevye's second daughter, happens by. Seeing and understanding that the milkman was trying to put money over love, Perchik observes that "money is the world's curse."

To this, Tevye stands up, points his hand heavenward, and yells firmly: "May I be smitten by it!" And then, with a second look up: "And may I never recover!"

Indeed, throughout this classic piece of Jewish literature, there is an underlying struggle with fate, with history, and the desire of the parents to help their children do better than they did. Tevye sings, "If I were a rich man . . ." His struggling dairy business, his lame horse, his ultimate poverty—are all parodied and lamented. Tevye wants his five daughters to have love and friendship. But he absolutely wants them to have money. The play is endearing to all of us, I think, because it finds a balance between the spiritual and the material. But Tevye is consistently and unabashedly committed to the financial well-being of his loved ones. As we see, he is certainly willing to strike a rather awkward nuptial deal for his daughter with a man who is absolutely inappropriate but does offer Tzeitel a lifetime of food and funds.

We should note that Tevye's daughters all eventually

wind up with more love and less money. Romance prevails in the story over wealth and circumstance. But, like it or not, the issue of money and its importance is pervasive, whether it's in Russia in 1905 or in America in the nineties. Money is important because civilization runs on it and because we simply have never devised any other means with which to structure society and to exchange goods and services.

Even though I have rarely met a teenager who actually disdains having some money to work with, I have heard the question raised: Why is money so important? The key word in this query is *so*. I don't think that any teenager really questions the importance of money; what's being examined is the potential *over-importance* of it. We adults need to find a way to make our children responsible to and for money, but to prevent them from feeling a poor sense of self-worth if their family isn't worth so much in dollars. Like Tevye the parent discovered, the answer for a child is somewhere in between finances and feelings. The way to negotiate the question of money is to realize the difference between value and values.

I'm always amazed when I visit one of the remaining communal settlements in Israel, known as a kibbutz. Israel, a fascinating and unique country, was really founded upon the kibbutz movement of this century. A kibbutz is a place where money is actually not the critical factor. Nobody really has any money of his own; all the families share equally in the productivity and ideology of the settlement. Israel is just about the only place where this has succeeded; a few attempts in North America over the years have pretty much failed. The fact is that, in the overwhelming number of human situations all over the world, people have struggled with and against each other to acquire the most money. The complete sharing of assets is an idealistic dream; such a notion certainly has little to do with the social structure of the United States. I am not proposing it, incidentally; America is still a free and open land where an ambitious, vigorous, and creative individual can and should achieve a fair measure of success. While discussing the portentous nature of money with a teenager, this last point should be stressed and appreciated.

But in a kibbutz, life is actually based upon ideology. The people who founded Israel were up against a hostile Arab population, the general indifference of the world, and an arid land that showed little evidence of productivity and usefulness. The kibbutzniks had little time for economic infighting and common jealousies. The Jewish population of British Palestine (which is what the area was from 1917 to 1948) did not have the resources and wherewithal to build a lot of capitalistic towns and villages. So, in many areas, they drew strength from one another, gave up the more typical exploitation that characterizes most communities, and decided to share everything.

Now, at the end of the century, with Israel prosperous, modern, and maybe even at the threshold of peace with its Arab neighbors, there aren't as many kibbutzim as there once were. Still, in a kibbutz, families all have similar dwellings and are allocated equal funds for living. If somebody wants to acquire a new television set or piece of furniture, a central committee decides what is appropriate. The members of the kibbutz do not generally have private automobiles; these are shared. People take turns working the kitchens, the fields, the industrial buildings. Everyone milks cows and collects the garbage in rotation. When a young man or woman wants to go to college or take a trip abroad, the kibbutz community works together to decide about it and to make the right allocations.

These remarkable communities are among few places on the face of the earth where money is not the central factor. In a kibbutz, people are valued evenly as opposed to being evaluated fiscally. These special settlements are still found throughout Israel, from the Galilee down to the Negev Desert. As against the greater scheme of things, these kibbutz villages are rare and unusual. But they do prove that people can live together in an idealistic environment. There is neither hunger nor poverty in such a community because every child starts out with the same things and nobody can take anything away from anybody else.

But, alas, America is not a kibbutz. We parents and professionals should have no illusions about this when we discuss money with our kids. America is no communal settlement. We are a sprawling land of subdivisions, commercial interests, major malls, and busy banks. We are heavily invested, and we are in a big hurry. Our cities are economic living units that look alike and are divided into successful suburbs and other sections euphemistically known as "enterprise zones." We are a dollar-driven society of fast-food cubicles and twenty-four-hour minimarts where a young governor from Arkansas was elected president mainly because he kept up the campaign refrain of "it's the economy, stupid."

No wonder teenagers sometimes ask why money is so important. They live in a culture based upon having, seizing, canning, and franchising. My real concern over this question is not so much that money is dangerous or evil. What strikes me about the question is that the overcommercialization of our country has perhaps made individual children feel less like people and more like digits. There's nothing wrong with a family having equity. There's a lot wrong with a family not having values. We parents must remember that when a kid comes home, he or she is coming in from an outside civilization that offers a limited regard for history, for language, for what some social critics call "a sense of place."

I knew this for sure one day while travelling along Eighty-sixth Street in Indianapolis, Indiana. Eighty-sixth Street is a linear thoroughfare, like so many such American pathways, totally saturated with bank machines, burger joints, self-serve fuel pumps, drive-through car washes and sundry superstores all selling the same commodities. This was Indianapolis but it could just as well have been Denver. The landscape offers the identical grid of franchises and food stations. You have everything you need but you are nowhere in particular; the common denominator is surely money and not meaning. This is the environment of every American teenager from Helena to Hoboken.

Money is so important because money has become not just our currency but also our culture. Successive cash registers, each housed in a structure-with-a-logo, are the coordinates of every teenager's life in a world where the mall has replaced Main Street. I think that a parent should understand and acknowledge what a teenager is up against. Our own generation might have been the last one where cash was certainly required and exchanged over the counter, but where somebody had a conversation with you instead of a security camera monitoring you.

These youngsters live in a new, clean and cold America. The service is great, the discourse is poor. So I thought I truly saw this new America one day, looking across Eighty-sixth Street in Indianapolis. Cooling off with my nonfat vanilla dessert at the Yogurt Crossing, I saw it through the window just across the way. There, shimmering in the light, in between Steak 'n Shake, Mountain Jack's, Vision Values, Jiffy Lube, Loew's multiplex and the automatic Amoco Fill and Wash, was the Chinese restaurant building with mauve highlights and the neon inscription THE FORBIDDEN CITY EXPRESS "Chinese Food in an Elegant Atmosphere."

If there is one thing I believe in, it's for every youngster to be well-informed and intellectually stimulated. History, for example, is a wonderfully edifying element of any teenager's student life. It broadens one's horizons and effectively curtails prejudice by illuminating the human experience. A great deal of good comes, for example, when a midwestern kid deals with something as exotic and fascinating as Far Eastern history. But now, on Eighty-sixth Street in Indianapolis, crammed in between Taco Bell and Rally's Burgers, the emperor of China had arrived—on the wings of a drive-through egg roll.

It just so happens that Emperor Yung-lo's Forbidden City was built centuries ago as an eternal palace to fight off regional barbarians, bad spirits, and hungry ghosts. This sublime bit of Chinese lore deserves a better treatment than it's getting for quick change and an order of Mongolian beef with scallion (item #43). The Forbidden City of

China, rich with tradition and mystery, was approached through Tiananmen Square, the "path of heaven." Forbidden City Express, late of America, is approached via a traffic light that controls access in-between Ditch and Michigan Roads. It's a decent enough eating place where you need your wallet but you do not need your mind; it's the strip culture of today's teenager: Capital, yes; chronicles, mythology, theology, necrology, and piety, no. It's small wonder why teenagers focus on money. It's the one and only thing out there that can operate any of these endless, cybernetic facilities that feed, clothe, and entertain these youngsters for whom even the Forbidden City has been converted into an express line.

So, before dealing with a teenager's question about money, we should place him or her directly into the middle of this fast-food decade. On the other hand, we should recall that the world has always run on silver and gold and that this reality offers both opportunity and responsibility. Apparently even God thinks that people can gain some insight by spending some money.

In the latter sections of the Book of Exodus, the Hebrews are exhorted to build a sanctuary for their desert devotions. This portable facility would be the advance model for the eventual, central Temple in Jerusalem. The instructions for this sanctuary are elaborate and complicated; the process of building and caring for it will help transform these former slaves into a free and responsible people of faith. It must be noted, however, that God required a contribution from everyone in the desert "with a willing heart." (Even God knows that you can't separate a donor from his money unless he believes in the project.)

In chapter twenty-five of Exodus, God tells Moses: "Speak to the children of Israel, that they may take for Me an offering. . . . And this is the offering that you shall take of them: gold and silver and brass. . . ." Indeed, later in Exodus, the question of silver donations was clarified, indicating a levy of a half-shekel upon each adult Israelite. While the gathering of precious materials and funds was necessary for the construction of the sanctuary, there was also another reason for the half-shekel donations: In real life, people are more "invested" in something if they participate financially. There is nothing wrong or underhanded about this; it represents a very positive manifestation of the importance of money. This is particularly true, as we have indicated, when the money is brought for an obviously meritorious project (for example, a church or a school) by people, as the Bible notes, "whose hearts are willing."

Given that money is so endemic to our culture, it is very appropriate for parents to discuss it with their children. There are plenty of fine causes that require money; teenagers and their families are solicited regularly by a variety of agencies. I am sometimes concerned by the approach taken when somebody comes along to ask children for a donation. To make a contemporary youngster feel guilty because his or her parents are comfortable is not the appropriate manner to approach this: "Kids like you are starving right here in America! How can you sit back and not care while being so well fed?!"

I think most teenagers are very able to care about hunger, for example, if they are taught properly and fairly about the problem. I think that such a discussion can bring about a better value system, thereby transferring the issue of money from the express line to the line of willing hearts. I think that inflicting guilt upon young people because they are blessed with material good is gratuitous and hypocritical. In a land soaking with money but quite devoid of compassion, we need to inspire young people not to feel badly that they have, but to feel better about sharing.

Why is money so important? In a way, this is like looking at a building and inquiring about the bricks. The question really is about the morality of money. I confess that I ask myself this question when people I serve as rabbi spend thousands upon thousands of dollars on a milestone religious ceremony. When two young people are in love, and they come to be blessed with matrimony, how does that translate into a discussion about paté and wines? I'm not against a wonderful wedding feast; I'm just more in favor of a bountiful human commitment.

In my religious community, there has been much discussion of late about the gaudiness of bar and bat mitzvah banquets. The situation has seemed to have gotten somewhat out of hand. This simple milestone, when a child blesses the Torah publicly for the first time and when his or her parents are moved to the knowledge that their youngster is now responsible to his or her tradition, is often reduced to a stereophonic blast of party music and a dreadfully dripping buffet line. I certainly am pleased to know that any member of my congregation is well-off enough to fete his or her child. I am just even more pleased when a parent draws his or her gratitude for that child more so from the book of life than from a book of checks. Even more gratifying for everybody involved, particularly for the young man or woman who is coming of age, are deliberate acts of kindness done at the time of bar or bat mitzvah celebrations in favor of society's countless hungry, homeless, and lonely. A little less pastry and a lot more charity will do everybody some good in an era when even grace has wound up in the express line.

For teenagers learning about money, I believe in earned allowances, part-time jobs and, whenever possible, in savings accounts. A young man or woman who is part of a family and who wants things should have a stake in building the sanctuary of life. Meanwhile, no youngster should be begrudged material well-being; he or she should just appreciate it. Tell your child that money itself is not the important problem. The problem has to do with the hands holding the money, especially if those hands are not connected to a good and willing heart.

CHAPTER 12

Why Does My Generation Get Stuck With All the Problems and Diseases of the World?

Whenever a teenager asks me the above question, or something in a similar vein, I thank him or her for being aware enough of the world's troubles to resent them. In the course of my response, I also tend to mention Dr. Martin Luther King, Jr., wondering out loud with the youngster about what might have *not* happened if someone like Dr. King had simply shrugged off the immense obstacles of his time.

If Dr. King had only lamented the problems that his generation inherited, would there have been any social change in the South? What would have become of all the segregated drinking fountains and public waiting rooms and dining counters that kept people apart from each other just because of the color of their skin? What about all the graduating high school seniors who—before Dr. King's time—

could not even think of attending certain colleges just because these students were born black?

Wouldn't the world be different today if King had simply given in to his own reluctance for the limelight and his understandable desire to just enjoy his wife and children? What would have happened if Dr. King and others like him had just settled on being "stuck"? If Dianne Feinstein and Barbara Boxer had not fought to become the first pair of female senators from California simultaneously elected, wouldn't we all still be somewhat stuck in a federal patriarchy? If a boy like Ryan White had just given in to being stuck with AIDS, and the bigotry it aroused in his Indiana classmates and their parents who wanted Ryan to move away, wouldn't his eventual death have taught us all a lot less than it did a few years ago?

There are many heroes in history who have been heroic because they did not dwell on these questions. They have understood that challenge and dilemma are as much the progression of history as children are the offspring of parents. No generation actually gets "stuck" with the problems of the previous one. The world has been spinning with pretty much the same categories of ailments, hindrances, ordeals, and bad habits from the beginning. The Romans were the Nazis of their time; Noah could have built his ark in the Iowa flood waters of 1993; AIDS is the equivalent of the medieval Black Death; murder is as old as the Bible and as new as this morning's metro news section.

In fact, the Bible asserts that "there is nothing new under the sun." Specific generations may have specific challenges, but ultimately human beings have always laughed, cried, bled, succeeded, failed, threatened, or uplifted each other. There has always been hunger and poverty and there has certainly always been injustice. People may dress differently than before, and they may even kill differently. But people are still born from their mothers and they still die with the last closing of their eyes. The threat of nuclear extinction does not make you or me any less mortal than we would have been a century ago.

Again, a primary reason for a question such as the one that titles this chapter has to do with too much information. In all fairness, it's rather easy for teenagers to fall into a line of thinking that betrays a certain edginess about "all the problems and diseases of the world." After all, even though today's kids are generally healthier than those of previous generations (as discussed in chapter nine), they are more informed about negative issues than ever before. It may be hard for a teenager to draw a perspective on there being "nothing new under the sun" while he or she is bombarded with upsetting or frightening reports on the human condition.

But we have to be careful: There are times when this question must be discerned as an example of whining. Teenagers do not always make inquiries out of conviction; laziness, apathy, and detachment are attributes known to young people. When this is the case, a parent has every right to respond to this question in, say, the following way: "Why do I get stuck with all the dirty laundry and the unkempt shelves of your bedroom?" People transfer situations and problems to each other because we live together—on the same planet or even in the same house. The answer is not to dwell on being stuck. The answer is how to get unstuck, thus moving the world a little bit more forward than it was before you came along.

We have made a few allusions already in this chapter to the Bible. One of the most remarkable people I have ever read about was Joseph. Joseph's story fills up the final few chapters of the Book of Genesis. It is a story of how a young man deals with a great deal of adversity and hardship—without ever looking up and complaining to God or anybody else. In fact, God is never particularly referred to in the whole story of Joseph. It's an account of how a human being realizes that he has inherited a number of problems and how he calls upon something inside himself to help solve these problems. I like the story of Joseph because it tells me some good things about how to live.

Joseph is separated from his family, is sold as a slave, and winds up in an Egyptian prison. He might have perceived himself as being the victim of the times in which he lived, as well as his family's poor emotional history. To read the story is to surmise that Joseph got stuck with other people's problems and lack of vision. But Joseph did not dwell on this; he pulled himself out of his predicament with savvy, creativity, and a lot of guts. He stood up for himself and wound up as the second most powerful person in Egypt. He also saved Egypt from the effects of a general famine that was coming. Like Nelson Mandela of our era, Joseph did not acquiesce to the previous errors of others; he rose up and corrected them.

Hannah Senesh could have simply shrugged her shoulders at the vicissitudes of her life and era. She was a teenager living in times that were profoundly characterized by the problems of previous generations. The Second World War was, in many ways, a storehouse of the tensions and faults of several prior decades—even centuries. Hannah Senesh was only seventeen when she decided to leave a comfortable and elegant life in Hungary in order to pursue the study of agriculture and poetry in the Jewish section of Palestine.

Among other things, Hannah felt that the Jewish people, so desperately under siege in Europe, needed to save their holy language. She learned Hebrew and eventually wrote poetry in it. But she and some of her young companions in Palestine began to understand that the war also brought with it the mounting genocide of the Jews in Europe. Now far removed from the luxurious life she knew back in Hungary, she joined a few others and parachuted behind Nazi lines in Yugoslavia. As a freedom fighter, her intent was to rescue as many people as possible from the Holocaust. She never stopped to bicker with fate and to wonder why her generation had inherited this terrible predicament.

In a bitter irony, Hungarian police captured Hannah Senesh. She was brutally tortured; the Nazis wanted information and a certain secret radio code from the comely, determined, and heroic youngster. They even located Hannah's mother in Hungary and brought her to the prison so as to deepen the torment. Hannah never relented. Instead, the accounts tell us that she wrote more poetry about Israel in prison and inspired others with her courage and resiliency. Even some of the prison guards were affected enough by this remarkable young woman to supply her with paper and material for her educational puppet shows and lectures given for her fellow inmates.

Late in 1944, the Nazis executed Hannah Senesh. She refused a blindfold and looked straight into her fate. Some of her poetry lives on in Jewish prayer books; this young woman is certainly enshrined as a hero among all decent peoples. What is hard to fathom is that she was not much more than a teenager when she absolutely defied the worst impulses of her own and every previous human generation.

I understand why a teenager might ask the question, "Why does our generation get stuck with all the problems and diseases of the world?" But this is a question that, frankly, a young person should not get away with. I shudder to think what might have been, say, if the kids in the Warsaw Ghetto had just muttered this question in 1943. In that desperate case, at least the Nazis were given a taste of their own blood. Virtually all the Jews still died, but the brief revolt brought some dignity into the neighborhood of hell. This is an extreme example, even as Hannah Senesh was extremely bold, but we must not let any generation of young people give in to the ramifications of this question. We must look, listen, and love, and then pray that these kids will rise to the occasion of the twenty-first century, for surely there is a Hannah Senesh or a Martin Luther King among them.

CHAPTER 13

Why Are Some People Gay?

Years ago, while in college, I had the good fortune of being cast in a musical that was being performed in a rather well-known local theater. It was quite an honor to join the company of Cincinnati's Showboat Majestic; shows performed there were reviewed in the local media and were considered to be professional-level productions.

The director was a jovial, experienced man of the stage who had a significant following in the Midwest. He encouraged me and took a special interest in my work, my problems, my life in general. When my father suddenly took ill during that period, my teacher was exceptionally kind and understanding. He let me pour my fears out, and spent many hours counseling and advising me. His was a most genuine and insightful shepherding during a difficult and transforming period of my youth.

One afternoon, prior to a performance, I waxed appreciatively about the teacher to some of my fellow student-actors in the dressing room. I noticed some snickering. "Don't you know why he's so nice to you?" chided one of my classmates. "He's gay, and he likes you! You're so naive."

The fact is I knew very well that my teacher was a gay man. I had even met the man he loved and with whom he shared his life. What his personal life had to do with the generosity of spirit he shared with me was immaterial to me. All he ever wanted to be to me was a very fine director who taught me a great deal about language, communication, and empathy. I understood, in that dressing room, that my fellow actors were flawed by bigotry, and that my teacher was the exact opposite of what they were.

A prominent American rabbi, Harold Schulweis, has written that "Judaism is married to reality, the whole of reality. It does not flinch from the encounter with sickness or death or guilt or sin. Nor does it avert its eyes from the condition of sexuality." It's true: The biblical and rabbinic literature is filled with candid discussions about lovemaking, reproduction, and personal behavior. Life is complicated; so is the biblical bearing towards homosexuality. On one hand, there is tolerance; on the other hand, there is hostility. In this ambivalence is a summary of human attitudes about gay and lesbian people and just about everything else. I shall examine some of what the Bible offers about homosexuality later in this chapter; there is an astonishing variance found between, for example, the books of Leviticus and Samuel.

Meanwhile, I can't help but think about the words of two modern teenagers in two different situations that help to define the contemporary ambivalence about people who are homosexual. The first, Terri, a fifteen year old, rented the video version of the motion picture *Philadelphia*, starring Tom Hanks. She brought it home on a Saturday evening and invited some friends over to watch with her. One of the friends inquired before coming over: "Isn't that the movie about AIDS?"

"Yeah, that's right," replied Terri, without a trace of malice. "The guy is gay, so he has AIDS."

None of us should think that Terri's summary is so far from the mainstream. Again, she was not being knowingly prejudicial, but her comments betray a lot of presumption about both the gay community on one hand and a virus shared across society's lines on the other. We need to remind our teenagers—who lump so many things together—that not everyone who is gay has AIDS and, even more importantly, not everyone who has AIDS has anything to do with the gay community.

"The guy is gay, so he has AIDS" is a terrible stereotype! Beyond that, by its tone, it releases any of us from responsibility in the matter of a devastating plague that is destroying the lives of so many young people who look just like you, me, and our children. Even if AIDS, or any other affliction, were strictly associated with the gay community, would it make the virus any less of a human tragedy? Before any of us with children begin to impart values, we had better sort out our own first.

My younger daughter, Debra, once asked me: "How do you feel about gay people, Dad?"

"How do you mean?" I retorted, truly curious.

"Would you want Sari or me to be lesbians?"

"Would I *want* you to be? No, because I don't exactly understand how lesbian love works, so I couldn't possibly relate to it well enough to be qualified to say it's great or the right thing for you. I know how I love Mom and how great that is, and so I want the same thing I know to be as wonderful for you."

"Doesn't your saying no make you prejudiced towards gay people?" continued my daughter.

"Not in the least, Debra. I honestly don't think so. In my answer—what is in my heart—is not prejudice against gays. I am biased *in favor* of heterosexual behavior because it's what I experience and it makes me happy and it gave me you and Sari. It's who I am, just like a gay person is who he or she is. You know, I don't care for pecan pie, but I have absolutely nothing against pecans."

"Okay, okay," said my inquisitive daughter. "But, Dad, let me ask you, what would you do if Sari or I were lesbians?"

"I would love you."

In this answer given to Debra is not only any parent's ultimate feeling about his or her child but also my recollection of somebody else's child—my second contemporary example. Michael, a teenager, was being prodded by his parents to go out with girls. He came to tell me that he felt awkward around a girl. He also told me about the cruel treatment he was getting from both boys and girls in his high school because of his lack of social ability. Childhood is not so innocent, nor devoid of the meanest instincts of adulthood!

Neither is the Bible without its harshness in this category. When Michael, who is gay, came to me, I immediately hoped that he had never read the twentieth chapter of Leviticus, where it is written: "And if a man lies with mankind both of these have committed an abomination. They shall surely be put to death. Their blood shall be upon them." Not only did I hope Michael had never read this selection, but I also was forced to hope he had never attended a traditional synagogue on Yom Kippur afternoon. That is because this verse is among those chanted during the public reading of the Torah on that most holy of afternoons—the afternoon of Judaism's extremely somber day of healing, penitence, and conciliation. Other sexual "abominations" are included in this strict Torah portion regarding human sexuality and morality (such as incest and adultery), but this young man would have surely only heard that section beginning with "Do not lie with a male as one lies with a woman. It is an abomination."

Michael was discovering something about himself that, yes, some people find abominable. Some of these same people are extortionists, liars, hypocrites, abusers, or other things that the Bible, in one place or another, labels as heinous. As a rabbi, I am well aware of things that men and women have done together that can only be construed as profane; the affection or intimacy between two men or two women will never be understood by everybody but should be unconditionally condemned by nobody except a fundamentalist who is truly certain of his or her own state of perfection.

The truth is that the Bible is a library of ideas, stories, and notions, many of which contradict one another. Even the initial story of creation appears in two versions in Genesis. The four Gospels live together in the New Testament but offer some widely variant details about the life of Jesus. Any parent, for example, who is certain that the Bible is single-minded about homosexuality had better reconsider (as we shall see). When a youngster like Michael is confronting himself, a parent needs to lift his or her eyes from an old text and gaze into the much newer eyes of that child who needs understanding at a critical time indeed.

Michael has been lucky. Now eighteen, he wrote a letter to his parents during his freshman year at college. "I know you were always disappointed that I didn't go to the prom or bring you home a high school sweetheart, but I'm sure you'll be much happier to know that I've just always been myself." Of course, it took the considerable distance between Michael's dormitory room and his parents' house to give him the courage to write his letter of revelation. His parents, however, who were not so surprised, bridged that distance quickly. They arrived at the university within two days with not too much comment and a lot of love. "He passed through me first," says his mother.

There is a Bible in Michael's room. I suspect that he and his very supportive family believe in its ultimate message while knowing that the writers of this great literature were—like most people today—doing the best they could.

"For my parents dealing with me," says Bruce, "it was not always unconditional love." The soft-spoken, meticulous musician, in his early forties, speaks about his sexual orientation with composure and forbearance. The fact that Bruce is director of music at Cleveland's Tifereth Israel, one of the most historic temples in the world, speaks positively about the growing tolerance that characterizes more and more social and religious institutions.

I tell Bruce that one of the teenagers who was asked to submit questions for this book had inquired about why some people are gay. "Homosexuality," he says, "is a natural variation of human sexuality. Nobody really knows exactly why some men are gay and some women are lesbian. It's possibly genetic or as a result of some other trait."

But what Bruce wanted his parents to understand starting over twenty years ago is that it is not "wrong." Bruce is a remarkably well-adjusted and successful individual with a wide range of professional interests. He lives in a comfortable and attractive house, filled with wooden furniture and quiet dignity. "Coming out," he explains, "is an expression of integrity. I just want the other person to know all of me. It also allows me personal freedom. . . . No more secrets, no shame, no control over me by something or someone else out there."

But Bruce is not strident. He is what he is, and wishes the same inner peace for anybody else. He has no illusions that gays and lesbians are perceived in different ways by different people. "Look," he tells me, "prejudice is so much a part of life. If it's not us, it's the Jews, black people, somebody else. If there weren't gays and lesbians, we'd probably invent another group to hate."

"What should parents say to their children about this?" I ask Bruce.

"Well, like with anything, keep the lines of communication open. In general, no parent should offer any discriminatory words about homosexuals. And certainly, the question of AIDS should not be automatically assumed to be a question of sexual preference. AIDS affects a lot more people than just gays and lesbians."

I focused my question on Bruce. What should happen, I wondered, when a parent comes to understand that his or her child is evidently homosexual? While Bruce has measured answers to this question in general, he clearly carries a specific pain in this category.

"When I told my parents, it was difficult. They went through a period of denial that, in some ways, continues. There are still issues. But I do think that the world is more open now, over twenty years later, and that people are better equipped with information and tolerance."

It can't be that easy for parents, I thought to myself, while admiring Bruce's honesty. Most parents are innately geared for their children's heterosexual dating activities, for the sexual tensions of high school homecoming, proms, and going steady. We contemplate weddings involving a bride and a groom, and we certainly think about the eventual appearance of grandchildren who will reassure us of a certain immortality.

But what if, I realized, one's child simply has a different sexual orientation? What about Michael? What about Bruce? "He passed through me first," says one of the finest mothers I have ever known.

"You have to reassure your gay or lesbian child of your continued love," says Bruce to me, quietly. "You have to be honest about your feelings, but do not accuse. Give it time. Work on your negative feelings. Above all, parents shouldn't focus on 'what we did wrong.' Think more about 'where do we go from here?' "

Bruce tells me about an important support organization (about which he has informed his parents) called P-FLAG. The Federation of Parents and Friends of Lesbians and Gays was created in 1979 and now includes over 270 chapters, according to the author Betty Berzon. In her book, *Positively Gay*, Dr. Berzon writes:

Geared to the individual needs and concerns of parents, [P-FLAG] has been successful in eradicating the sense of isolation, the grief and pain, the guilt feelings and the fear, hostility and anger that many thousands of parents have experienced and helping them understand what being gay or lesbian means to their children and to others.

Bruce and I are both creatures of the synagogue, so the talk inevitably turns to Torah—the biblical literature. I have no doubt that Bruce knows the harsh decrees of Leviticus, but wonder out loud if he recalls the love poetry of the First Book of Samuel. It seems as though David, the future king and messianic leader of Israel, has a relationship with Jonathan, son of King Saul, that is more than a boyhood fancy.

Bruce smiles as he tells me: "The deep connection described in the Bible between Jonathan and David means a lot to people like me." Bruce proceeds to recall a visit he made to his family's Conservative synagogue several years ago. His mother and father were with him; the family was still working hard to adjust to the reality of Bruce's sexual orientation. There they were, in the pews of a traditional house of worship. In many ways, the atmosphere of such a place would be unwelcoming to a gay or lesbian person. It was a potentially unsettling time for Bruce.

An irony occurred when it came time for the weekly reading from the Prophets, known as the Haftarah. Bruce experienced a wonderful sensation of relief and gratitude as he heard the opening phrase chanted from the First Book of Samuel. Jonathan, the son of King Saul, was addressing his dear and close friend, David: "And Jonathan said unto him: 'Tomorrow is the new moon, and thou wilt be missed, because thy seat will be empty.' "

I myself remember first reading this biblical story as a teenager. I went to my mother, a Hebrew school teacher, wondering about the strong bond between David and Jonathan. My mother responded, matter-of-factly: "What do you mean? They were homosexuals!"

Indeed, this unfolding drama in the Book of Samuel clearly indicates a passionate relationship between these two young heroes. The romantic pressure between them was particularly poignant as against the prevailing tension of the story: Jonathan's father, King Saul, was insanely paranoid about David because David was considered by many to be the true heir apparent to the throne. Saul wanted to eliminate David, and once even threw a spear at the boy. Jonathan, the genetic heir apparent, was nonetheless fiercely loyal to his friend—in spite of his father's disapproval and the fact that David's general popularity in the kingdom could very well deny the throne to Jonathan himself. Here, in the same canon that contains the edicts of Leviticus, is an intense saga of power, rivalry, and Oedipal complexes all being driven by the force of homosexual love. My mother was right a long time ago when she understood the deeper implications of Jonathan feeling "empty" when David's chair was vacant.

But the Bible does not exactly mince words about the whole thing, either. In the twentieth chapter of 1 Samuel, it describes an outdoor reunion between the two boys. At a point of rendezvous, "David arose out of the place toward the South, and fell on his face to the ground, and bowed down three times; and they kissed one another, and wept one with another, until David exceeded."

The final phrase of this very descriptive verse, "until David exceeded," might very well give some people a measure of trouble. It is interpreted by some biblical critics as an explanation of David's intense crying—that is, he ran out of tears. The fact is that the literal translation of the Hebrew is "until David enlarged." One can have no illusions about what the Bible is describing in this particular instance.

David went on to an illustrious career as monarch, psalmist, and empire builder. Christians and Jews alike ascribe messianic aspects to his life and his person. He certainly came to love many women as a grown man, but the Bible is broad enough and honest enough to include his youthful dalliance with another young man in his biography. Does this mean that the Bible is in favor of homosexuality? I think what it means is that even the Bible recognizes many attitudes and that this should teach us not to be, among other things, homophobic.

Meanwhile, Jonathan's rather sad life ended early and violently. Along with his father, King Saul, Jonathan died in battle. It was, of course, David who wrote the eulogy for both of these men, adding the following stanza especially for his fallen lover:

> *O, Jonathan, slain upon the high places,*
> *I am distressed for thee, my brother Jonathan;*
> *Very pleasant hast thou been unto me:*
> *Thy love to me was wonderful,*
> *Passing the love of women.*

Why are some people gay? For the same reasons that some other people are not.

CHAPTER 14

Is My Religion
Really the Truth?

Sometimes, it is easy to wonder what God must think about all the arguing going on in the world about religion. One would imagine that God wants religion to be something satisfying and unifying, not divisive and dangerous. Many youngsters have pointed out to me that more people have been killed in the name of religion than were ever saved by it. No one has any definitive statistics about this, but neither can anybody dispute that religious issues have generated a great deal of trouble between people—from the contested holy sites of Israel, to the street corners of Northern Ireland, to the abortion clinics of the United States.

This question is a powerful and meaningful one, and the way in which a parent deals with it can reveal something in itself about how religion has affected that parent.

But teenagers think a lot about God, and they tend to view religion with somewhat of a skeptical eye: They are perhaps more convinced of adult hypocrisy in this category than in almost any other. They are generally unimpressed with the obsessive hold that any one religion may have over any individual, regarding a fierce loyalty to one's faith as coming with a built-in bias against another. This is an open and disputatious society; God's advocates are either trying to convince others to "come together" or to really lash out against those who are too stupid or too "unsaved" to know the truth!

I am basically suspicious about the tendency towards extreme talk in the matter of God, and feel a special concern for young people trying to sort it out. Life is scary and confusing enough without a group of radical grown-ups trying to dictate divinity to kids while holding a Bible in one hand and a threat in the other.

A special perspective on which religion is the truth was once offered by someone who has an intrinsic right to view God critically—Elie Wiesel. Wiesel, often known as the poet laureate of the Jewish people, is perhaps the best known survivor of the Holocaust. As a young man during those horrifying years, Elie Wiesel lost his family, his friends and, for a time, his soul. No one has described the insanity of the genocide with more searing and unforgiving candor than this remarkable and gentle writer and teacher.

Elie Wiesel was the featured guest on a panel some years ago. The community forum dealt with the issues of Holocaust, survival, and hope; I was privileged to be a participant on the dais. Towards the end of the program, we panelists were permitted to ask Wiesel questions for the audience to hear. All evening, as I sat next to him, I observed the deep lines of experience and suffering that are woven into Elie Wiesel's face. Looking into his eyes is a mystical experience; these are wells of permanent pain that nonetheless convey a certain, tortured belief in the future of humankind. Elie Wiesel is soft-spoken, wiry, uncompromising in his demand for compassion between people. His very presence in a room, and the soothing timbre of his voice, are the quiet evidence that Hitler didn't kill everything.

When my turn came to ask him a question, I inquired: "Professor Wiesel, after the war ended and you were finally freed from the concentration camps, when was the first time that you were able to smile again?"

The Nobel laureate paused momentarily, but then he raised his eyebrows in recognition of a restored memory. "Yes," he said, his face lifted slightly higher than before. "I recall the moment."

Dr. Wiesel proceeded to recount a long walk he took within a year or so of the close of the war. It was along a rural road in France—where he has subsequently spent a fair amount of time. He explained that, as he made his way along the road, he thought he heard the sound of singing voices. He then realized that he was approaching a country church. Wiesel, who was persecuted by the Nazis because of his Jewish background, felt drawn to the doorway of the abbey. Inside, he gazed at and heard an exuberant group of children singing together under the busy direction of their choirmaster. "They were beautiful children," he said, his eyes watering. "They sang like angels, in Latin. There was a pure and simple joy about them. I did not understand the words of their liturgy but I felt the utter truth of their expression. It was then, at that moment, that I felt myself breaking into a smile again for the very first time."

It was a breathtaking report that naturally moved every person present at that forum. Its impact was deepened because Elie Wiesel himself seemed truly transformed; indeed, as the audience finished a spontaneous burst of applause, he added that he hadn't truly thought of that breakthrough since it happened more than a generation earlier.

I often recall this special moment with Elie Wiesel. It seems to me that his memory says something about faith and truth. There is no doubt that Wiesel's small epiphany represented a spiritual threshold. It was not just the sound of the children's voices that lifted his spirits, he explained. It was the "utter truth" of their devotions—coming in the aftermath of his own wretched childhood experiences in the world of absolute falsehood. The fact that Wiesel—a Jew who has written extensively about Jewish sources and sages, and who has reaffirmed his spiritual identity after living through the near-death of God—could be so transfixed in that little French church indicates that there is an element of basic truth for everyone in every religion when that religion is unimpaired by indoctrination. What God wouldn't have taken pleasure in the sound made by such children in the countryside?

It's good and important for young people to have a religious identity, but we have to be careful when we ascribe absolute truth to this or that doctrine. We each need a religion in the same way that a language needs grammar. I am thoroughly satisfied with my Jewish heritage. I would only pray that this inner peace would not prevent me from experiencing a transcendent moment like Wiesel did just because I was standing inside somebody else's church. After all, it was not God who wrote the various religious contracts of our life. It was people.

The potential problem with kids and religion in our civilization is that the civilization is built on the foundation of ethnic advantage. Everybody's faith system requires validation, expression, and in many cases, public holidays and heritage weeks to be shared by one and all. The basic instinct here is noble and decent: My religion is good and worthy. The secondary instinct, too often unleashed, is not so valorous: My religion is true and yours is false. Again, as I mentioned in chapter six, we are too often obsessing about ethnic differences when we should be celebrating ethnic qualities.

This public bickering about theological issues does little for the private disposition of a youngster's soul. When is religion true? When is my religion the truth? I learned some of the answers to all of this from a young girl named Jessie.

Jessie, now fifteen, is in an increasingly large category of contemporary youngsters who have parents of different religious backgrounds. Jessie's mother was raised Catholic and her father is Jewish. These factors, while complicated, have not prevented the family from enjoying a beneficent spiritual life both at home and in the temple that I serve. Both Jessie and her younger sister, Nora, have celebrated their ceremonies of Bat Mitzvah in the congregation.

But Jessie—to her great credit—did not simply comply

with the process of becoming a Bat Mitzvah, which means *daughter of the commandments*. Unlike many youngsters whose parents are both Jewish, Jessie did not fall in line because this is what happens when you're thirteen years old. The irony is that, when the religious question in a family is not controversial, good questions are sometimes not asked. Why should I do this? What does it really mean? If the rabbi gives me a blessing, isn't that something important? Is there really more to this than a big party in the evening? Doesn't this really mean that I have a commitment to my religion?

Jessie has a lot to think about, and, fortunately for her family and her religious community, she does think. Her house is quite an egalitarian place; the door is open and a lot of people drop by for a variety of festivals ranging from the Jewish New Year to Chanukah to Christmas to Passover to St. Patrick's Day. Jessie's mother prays in our temple but holds fast to her Irish-Italian background. Eileen is an energetic, caring, and gregarious human being who is a nurse-practitioner, social activist, and quintessential neighbor. She is a genuine liberal who actually likes people as much as she loves humanity. There just isn't a false note about this woman. I can't imagine that God finds anything lacking about her devout commitment to the human family.

Jessie's dad, Barry, a psychologist, has gentle hands and a soft voice. Having grown up partially as a foster child, he sees the world through unusually sympathetic eyes. A sincere and kind man, he turns for healing to his Judaism at moments when life is brutal. The fact that Eileen and Barry adopted Jessie adds to the challenging set of emotional and theistic issues that sometimes besiege this typical-looking suburban family of four people, a dog, a minivan, and a portable cellular telephone.

But is this mix of heritages ultimately a good thing for Jessie? As with most things, I see plusses and minuses inherent in the situation. If there is love in the house, then I am not ultimately worried about the folks involved. Naturally, I am committed to the perpetuity of a single religious faith in the families that I serve, but I am even more committed to the inner peace of any child or adult who happens to come into my temple looking for God.

So, I was not threatened or upset when Jessie told me, in the months before her Bat Mitzvah ceremony, that she wasn't sure about being Jewish or Catholic. Frankly, the Bible that I cherish is filled with the accounts of people struggling with their theological dilemmas. Truth is often better carved out of a quest than it is from quiet. I wish that more teenagers would be inspired, for genuine reasons, to grapple with God; it would certainly help to turn their milestone religious experiences from materialism to morality.

Now, one response from parents that I do not find so helpful is the following: "We will have our child go to both temple and church and then let her choose when she's eighteen." I feel for the youngster left in that kind of confusing, if well-meaning entanglement. Kids need to know what beliefs their parents share! In a world of so many distractions and too many choices, the home is the one place where a youngster should feel some unanimity and agreement. We don't always let them pick their clothes or their cars by themselves; why leave the choice of their inner life left to such serendipity? In the category of God, a child needs to feel that there is at least a consensus in the family on what will serve as the truth.

Jessie went to church as a child, and she was also exposed to Jewish places and holidays. But her parents worked closely with her, talked with her, emoted with her. Eileen and Barry, cognizant that their daughter was searching for truth, also studied each other's backgrounds in order to keep the whole process honest and open. In short, Jessie was guided to her ultimate decision in a way that would make her choice informed. She was not simply left on her own to do some ecclesiastical window-shopping. Eileen was evidently not as committed to Catholicism as Barry was to Judaism; a harmony developed in the household as to where the two daughters would eventually meet with God. As a rabbi, I submit that all of this does not just represent some kind of political "victory" for Judaism. No, the winner is Jessie, and the spoils have to do with the young girl's soul. Religious truth is not just what some men wrote down a long time ago. The truth is what you feel when you find peace as a result of any good combination of God, the writ, and what your parents and grandparents have passed along to you.

When Jessie arrived for her Bat Mitzvah ceremony, she came with the windows of her soul open. After years of thought and support, she had consciously decided that this was right for her. She set aside her childhood baptism, and she neutralized what she describes as the frightening sight of a church God "hanging from a cross with blood dripping down his body." She also fought through her fears of the Holocaust, affirming that she was proud, not scared, of being part of a people who have been so persecuted yet so resilient. For the first time, Jessie put on a Star of David that shone on her chest. In this case, the star was not just a piece of jewelry. It was an affirmation of truth as this demanding and pensive young woman perceived it.

I remember so well when I blessed this girl with the star. Her eyes absolutely shimmered with tears—the salty waters of her spiritual homecoming. Later, I would ask her: "Jessie, why do you think you were crying at the close of the ceremony?"

"Because it was all there, the love and the warmth, the feeling that God was right there, through your words to me. I felt like one person."

Not every child, of course, is as uniquely challenged or as eventually inspired as Jessie. But most every teenager wonders about the validity or sanctity of his or her religion. In most schools, a number of religious traditions are taught and discussed. It is fashionable to ascribe righteousness and respect for other faith systems; in general, the barriers between groups have been broken down in our postmodern culture. On the other hand, Jewish parents are often anxious about the proliferation of Christmas symbols and images that rise every December, or about the new talk and pressure for prayer in school. There is a fundamentalist coalition out there; its advocates don't pretend to regard the United States as anything but a purely Christian land that happens to have other kinds of inhabitants in it. One way to deal with all of this religious righteousness is to immerse your own child in the genuine gladness and fulfillment that your family religion has given you. My daughters visit other families who share Christmas with them. Sari and Debra—like Jessie—know their own religion well enough and happily enough to be able to enjoy somebody else's beautiful holiday without being threatened by it.

Every parent has the right and the responsibility to preserve his or her family heritage through the children. The stories of Elie Wiesel and of Jessie may serve to teach that "truth" in religion is not an absolute thing as much as it is an acquired quality. You can't and you shouldn't legislate truth to your child. You should nurture and inspire it through your own commitment to the faith of your family. You certainly should mix a lot of love into the prayers. You should let your child explore the tenets of other faiths because a satisfied curiosity lends a warm foundation to a youngster's ultimate peace of mind. In the end, the answer to the question, "Is my religion really the truth?" lies in the fact that your youngster is already calling it "my religion." He or she isn't asking you this question out of a need to deny your religion. He or she just wants to make sure that the religion in question does represent the truth for you.

CHAPTER 15

Why Do I Have to Marry in My Own Race and Religion?

For some, it's easy: Their children are raised to view any other culture as anathema and there is a ban on any social interaction. This policy certainly exists among fundamentalist Jews (and corresponding sects in other religions) and it can be argued that the result is a certain ethnic continuity. What can also be argued, however, is that most young people are curious about the world around them and are apt, regardless of imposed habits, to want to find out about other people and their ways of life.

So what does a parent do? The question applies particularly to the parent who is filled with neither any social phobias nor an overwrought sense of messianic mission about his or her religious group. In other words, what's the reality in the three-dimensional America of the 1990s where Jews, for example, are intermarrying at a rate of about 52 percent? When you consider that in the metropolitan Denver area, the rate is almost 75 percent (it's quite high in a number of sections of the country), then, in a sense, the above question is somewhat redundant.

Before setting out on this difficult, even painful subject, I wish to offer a perspective that is important to me as both a parent and a rabbi. While every ethnic group deals urgently with its own continuity, the Jewish people have something that no other group has in the more immediate context: The twentieth century burden of the Holocaust.

I lived for a time as a child in Israel. While there are still survivors of the Nazi insanity in many places, their immediate impact upon others is perhaps felt most keenly in the Jewish state. This was even more so a generation ago, when former inmates of the camps were then young parents in a land that defied what the Nazis had intended.

Some of my fourth grade classmates at the Usshishkin School in the village of Kfar Saba in 1961 were the children of Holocaust orphans. The notorious Adolf Eichmann, a creator and leader of the Final Solution, was being tried for his crimes against humanity within our small and still fledgling country. His would be the only capital punishment ever carried out in Israel; the whole episode was much more frightening to us youngsters than it was edifying.

I think that we got more of a sense of the sanctity of survival from being around the numerous witnesses and sufferers who lived among us. They were parents, bus drivers, ice cream vendors, and booksellers. Indeed, Old Man Binstock, who owned the town bookstore in the village square, had survived Dachau. His gray shop, where we purchased our school texts and notepads, always had that dusty-sweet smell of old tomes and wisdom. Binstock, a cheerful man in spite of it all, was also part of an informal network of educators who recruited young Israelis to go abroad and teach Hebrew and Bible to Diaspora youngsters. One of his recruits, in 1962, would be my own mother. Each time Binstock successfully sent a teacher to the States or elsewhere for a term of instruction, he would tell patrons in his shop: "Another scoop of dirt in Hitler's grave."

And then there was Mr. Steiner. He was more mysterious than the others; we really never knew where he lived or what he did for a career. But in the fall of 1961, as we grade-schoolers resumed our studies, we noticed the tall, white-haired gentleman who met us most every morning outside the schoolyard gate. He was kind and sweet and, as we quickly learned, enjoyed eating sunflower seeds. It became a matter of pride for whomever among us little group of boys provided Mr. Steiner with his daily bag of fresh sunflower seeds. He was thankful for us in the morning, and, as the wind blew in the scent of the nearby orange groves and onion fields, he would gently tap each one of us on the top of our heads.

One can only imagine the legal and social implications of this daily visit and contact with a "stranger" anywhere in America over thirty years later. But in Israel in 1961, we were not afraid of a smiling older man who liked to chat with us young boys about autumn rain, soccer, and sunflower seeds. Although he never directly mentioned the Holocaust, we understood he had had something to do with it from two things: the tattooed numbers on his forearm and the phrase he often used when he, in fact, tapped our heads good-bye for the morning. Mr. Steiner would almost always say, looking into our faces and putting his wrinkled hand on us: "You're not number six million and one."

I refer to the tense grip of the Holocaust in the matter of marriage and ethnicity because history has simply too often created the dilemma. When Jewish people, for example, fret about their children marrying other Jews, they are not asserting their hope based upon a diminished capacity for non-Jews to give and receive love. No, the issue is survival of the group, plain and simple. For the Jews, this is a particularly anguished concern because the combination of six million murders (including 1.5 million kids) between 1933 and 1945, plus a noticeably high rate of intermarriage since the Holocaust, adds up to very poor arithmetic. Any teenager who is fair and reasonable should be able to understand that a parent who participated in the birth of Jewish children wants also to eventually hold Jewish grandchildren.

Nor is this desire for family continuity confined to Jewish circles. I have heard colleagues of mine in the African-American community express anxiety about the encroachment of the Nation of Islam upon and within their Baptist congregations. Italian-Americans and Irish-Americans want their children to speak the same cultural language that their grandparents did; this is as natural an expectation as the hope any person has for a healthy apple tree to blossom in the spot where he or she planted an apple seed.

And yet, all of us, Jewish, black, white, Irish, Italian, know that America is the intersection of so many tribal groups, and that our nation's educational framework is still largely based upon its public schools, and that we are ostensibly a national "melting pot." Only parents who segregate their children into certain types of protective and heritage-sanitized private schools have some kind of a line into ethnic purity. These parents, incidentally, have every right to place their children into whichever schools or social settings they prefer; I only suggest that our country is big and brimming with communal traffic. People meet each other and are sometimes even drawn to each other. Teenagers are especially susceptible to this and are not as cranky as their worried parents about the cultural implications.

I think a lot about the question raised that titles this chapter. The youngster who asked it speaks for many people of all ages. As with every good and penetrating question, the answer is complicated. But as both a rabbi and the parent of two young women who I hope will know love in their lifetimes, I find the matter timely and urgent. In responding to it, I wish to refer to two instances, one biblical and the other contemporary, that may offer some perspectives.

The Bible tells me a lot of things about people and reality. Again, the fact that this literature is flawed, even contradictory sometimes, draws me to it even more; life itself is usually more contradictory than it is perfect. In Deuteronomy there is a harsh ban on intermarriage between the Hebrews and the indigenous Canaanites of the land. But then the rabbinic tradition, in a much more magnanimous moment, declared about people: "And a single human being was created for the sake of peace, that none might say—'My lineage is greater than yours.'"

But the Bible itself seems to be filled with an egalitarian spirit about love and relationships. Prophets and monarchs do, in fact, intermarry; King Solomon of Judea certainly found something in common with the Queen of Sheba. In fact, this same Solomon—David's son—who built the Holy Temple in Jerusalem, spent a good deal of his time constructing pagan temples for the pleasure and appeasement of his assorted foreign wives. Granted, the Jewish tradition takes Solomon to task for his less than noble behavior in several categories, including lovemaking, adventuring, and tax levying. My point is, however, that even the Bible has different stories to tell about the human heart at various intervals in the text. One of the most notably intermarried prominent Jews of the Bible was none other than Moses himself.

One of the more poignant stories of Exodus is that of the fugitive Moses, who fled Egyptian justice after slaying a brutal taskmaster of slaves. Moses, looking for peace and safety, winds up in the hill country of Midian. There he falls in love with and weds Zipporah, the daughter of the Midianite priest, Jethro. Moses has a tender and satisfying relationship with this non-Hebrew woman who fathers his children and stands by him during the later adventures of the Hebrew exodus from Egypt. Moreover, the Bible takes pains to describe the strong affinity between Moses and his decidedly non-Jewish father-in-law, Jethro the priest.

Indeed, after the Hebrews have left Egypt, Moses finds himself overwhelmed by his new administrative duties as leader of the freedom march. Moses never sought this responsibility; he would have preferred his previous life as a shepherd in his wife's homeland of Midian. Now he is vexed and frustrated by the overwhelming requirements of leadership. It is his father-in-law Jethro who brings Moses some solace and reason. "You take too much upon yourself," says the priest. Jethro then suggests the development of a cadre of judges and ministers who would take the central burdens off Moses. Meanwhile, the fact that the very Torah portion from Exodus that includes the receiving of the Ten Commandments is entitled "Jethro" tells us that the Bible does not seem to draw a premium on the inherent wisdom and value of any specific ethnic group.

A young man once came to see me in my study. He had a wife and two small children, but his wife had betrayed him. The breach in the marriage had occurred several months before this consultation; the young man, Mark, came to discuss his life, his prospects, and, specifically, another young woman whom he now loved.

Mark came with an assumption that since his new sweetheart was not Jewish, I would disapprove. Again, while being committed to the continuity of my religious tradition, I am ultimately committed to the spiritual welfare of every congregant I serve. As far as marriage is concerned, the fact that two people are both Jewish does not guarantee their compatibility nor their appropriateness for a lifetime pledge. I have met many people in my study whose suitability for marriage was dubious. In some cases they shared the same faith and in some cases they did not. Beyond their religious backgrounds, people bring a number of factors to a potential union: maturity, integrity, a willingness to share the intricacies of human life with another person. Moreover, there are plenty of people I meet who are Jews in name only. Their commitment to raise Jewish children does not necessarily make an impression on me. The continuity of any ethnic group has to do with quality as well as quantity.

So, while I was not going to jump for joy that Mark had found himself a new romantic interest who did not share his religious faith, I certainly did not plan to become judgmental. But then Mark shared some thoughts with me that really made me think and that have enlightened me in my rabbinate ever since.

It has to be explained that Mark's former wife had become involved with someone else during the marriage, and that the revelation of this affair had caused particular pain and embarrassment to Mark and his family circle. Now, Mark's former wife was planning to marry her new partner, even as Mark came to me with his own new direction. Apparently, people in the Jewish community were expressing their poor opinion of Mark's plans, given that his new fiancée was not Jewish. Mark pointed out to me that people were not so critical of his former wife and her intended: "It seems that, just because they're both Jewish, what they did to both of the families involved—to my children—is simply overlooked. It's okay for them to get together because they're both Jewish. Meanwhile, the fact that now a loving and wonderful woman has come along and helped me feel like a person again, that she has helped me heal my wounds, and that I really and truly love and need her —all of this is insignificant just because this person happens not to be Jewish. I think there's a double standard here, Rabbi."

Granted, there was a certain level of subjectivity in

Mark's report and analysis of a very personal and intense situation. Nor is everybody in the Jewish community guilty of the biases conveyed in Mark's story, even as every Christian is neither totally enlightened nor benighted. But a basic truth struck home in the young man's passionate words. In this difficult and emotional matter of marriage and religion, we must never lose sight of the fact that a cultural group relies upon statistics, but a human being relies upon the heart.

Mark's astute plea made me wonder: Would some of the same critics he described have harassed Moses because of the leader's devotion to Zipporah? Could anybody be so cruel as to second-guess the warm and informative relationship between Moses and his father-in-law, Jethro? The love and support that Moses obviously received from his marriage family certainly did not prevent him from saving and delivering the Hebrew people to their new destiny. So, we can be committed to religious and cultural continuity; we can even demand it from others. But we must allow for some compassion and insight. Sometimes, certain people are inclined to help each other, or they are even meant to be together. A religion needs to survive, but what kind of religion is it without any tolerance?

The answer to a youngster's question about having to marry within his or her group requires a great deal of discussion and genuine examination. If you want your children to marry in your heritage, you have to provide real reasons. A teenager today is not going to buy into the argument that you do it just because you're supposed to do it. You need to display a certain, heartfelt involvement in that heritage —more than a passing interest in your own religious life and a few stilted statistics. If the Holocaust affects your soul, share this with your youngster. He or she is not defaming your religion by asking you to explain why it is so important to you that it continue. Every religious and cultural group in America—from Jewish to Serbian to Palestinian to African to Christian Scientist—can make a case in the newspaper for its continuity because so many people have died in this or that situation. These histories and these agonies are important and worthy of history. But what your youngster wants to hear when he or she asks you about being with other kinds of people is your explanation of what makes your religion worth living.

CHAPTER 16

Why Do Some Parents
Abuse Their Kids?

I want to tell you about a young person who asked me the above question without ever actually uttering it.

I enjoyed the fire in Saralyce's eyes from the first time we met—on a day when a large gathering of clergy, writers, psychologists, and teachers was convening in our temple to discuss the problem of sexual abuse in our society. I was the moderator of the daylong program, which a number of local students, including Saralyce, were going to observe.

The young woman, then in her senior year of high school, was coming down the stairway that leads from the main sanctuary of the temple to a lower floor that includes an auditorium. Her eyes met mine as we made our way, side by side, down the long stairwell.

"Am I going the right way to the seminar?" she asked.

I replied that she was. Sensing an uneasiness about her, I proceeded to welcome her and tell her who I was. As we came to the landing, she turned to me and asked, her eyes flashing: "Are you going to be performing a wedding up there in the sanctuary?"

I was, in fact, scheduled to officiate at a wedding that evening. The marriage canopy was already up, and she had obviously taken a look inside the sanctuary. There was something about Saralyce that suggested a yearning for *something*. I let her know that she was not only welcome to observe the coming discussion in the auditorium, but to remain afterwards and watch the wedding as well. "The two events are quite a contrast to each other."

"Not necessarily," she said, rather seriously.

I immediately got her point, that family relationships and sexual abuse are anything but separate matters. I understood that I was conversing with a very earnest young woman who had a great deal on her mind. She seemed, all at once, angry, curious, and in emotional pain. And she certainly was direct with some of her questions:

"So, Rabbi, are you going to have the groom break the glass during the wedding?"

"Yes, naturally," I answered, noting an edge to her inquiry.

"So will that make everybody think of the bride's hymen?" Saralyce was looking straight at me, absolute determination evident in the set of her jaw. This teenager appeared to have lived and experienced much longer than her still tender number of years. I was already as concerned about her as I was intrigued by her. Meanwhile, I was speechless, so she continued: "I mean, isn't that why the man breaks the glass at the end? To symbolize what happens when he penetrates the woman later?"

I cleared my throat and asked: "What makes you think *that* about the breaking of the glass?"

"Oh, don't get me wrong." Saralyce softened a bit. "I think it's a beautiful moment. When I see it, I feel for my religion and for the beauty of real love. I'm sure most everybody feels real love in those moments of a wedding ceremony. It's so painfully poetic, I guess, when he breaks the glass, and then everyone yells for them to have good luck. Such an innocence at that moment. . . ." Her voice trailed off a bit; I thought her eyes were a bit wet.

"Well, then," I offered. "Isn't that the point? What you feel at such an instant is exactly what it's all about."

Now, the teenager's deep eyes dried and hardened. "Oh, no, Rabbi. It's about her hymen. That's why it's all ultimately ruined for me. If I ever get married, I will refuse to allow my husband to commit such a barbaric act under the canopy. What's happened or what will be happening with my hymen is not for a public display."

It did not take a genius to figure out that this lonely girl coming to listen to a clinic on abuse was in deep agony. I did not know her well enough to presume anything, nor were we in a setting that was appropriate enough for me to speak directly to her about her obvious family wounds. That would come later; for now, I wanted to gain her confidence and trust. She, after all, had initiated the conversation, and the underlying plea, on her own.

"That moment at the wedding, when two people have just pledged themselves to each other, is not about the woman's hymen. Not one person coming into this temple, except perhaps some stray mystic hung up on such an idea, would even think of such a thing when the groom breaks the glass." A bitter, hoarse laugh exited from the girl. "There are a number of reasons why a person would think the way I do when a bride and groom stand there and he breaks the glass. But just a minute, Rabbi. I learned about this a long time ago. The sound of the wineglass symbolizes what I am describing."

"You learned about some superstitious carryover from another era. Every religion has this kind of baggage. You say that the moment does give you an exalted feeling. Try looking at the glass breaking in this way." Saralyce's eyes appeared damp again. I was desperate to keep a hold on her. I continued.

"The groom breaks the glass at the moment of the couple's supreme joy, when the rabbi has just declared them to be married. But right at that moment, at the dizzy heights of their happiness, the two are reminded by the breaking glass that joy is fleeting, that it's like a passing dream. This is the truth about life, just like your strong questions and your own experiences, good and bad, are true to life."

Saralyce quickly deflected my oblique reference to her private life. "Look," she said, "I've also heard that the groom breaks the glass to remind everybody about the fall of the ancient temple in Jerusalem. No matter what, a depressing tag seems to be applied to a moment that should be so spiritual."

"At least that's better than what you maintain about the hymen. But it just proves that even you are aware of more than one explanation. Yes, some people believe that the glass is broken to recall difficult moments in history. Frankly, I'd rather focus on something more redeeming concerning that moment. I'd like people to learn from love. So, when the marriage of two people has just begun, maybe the two of them will think of the bittersweet truth that life is precious, and that, like a glass, it can be broken. Now, let me ask you something: Are you here today, and are we talking like this because something in you feels broken?"

"Yes."

Pulling the young girl off to the side, away from the gathering crowd, I whispered to her: "Do you have something on your mind that has to do with the topic of this conference?"

"Yes."

"Will you let me talk with you some more?"

"You mean, alone?"

"It doesn't have to be. I mean, just talk."

"Okay. Maybe."

"Maybe we can talk a bit later today, when everybody is having lunch. If you want to, just walk over. Lunch is in the room next to the auditorium. I'll definitely be there because I love to eat! You can find me."

"Okay," said Saralyce. "I'll look for you." She walked away, wiping her glistening eyes with her bare hands.

At the lunch break, she came over to an empty seat next to me. Fortunately, I was not occupied with anyone else, and Saralyce resumed her interrogation:

"Rabbi, did you know that there is no biblical word for *bachelor*? No such word in old Hebrew. What kind of business is that? A man is not complete unless he's married, and then he's not certified unless he shatters some glass? You say this whole thing is about love, but I think it's about slavery."

"Saralyce, no matter what is ailing you, you can't tell me that love is about slavery because I happen to have a loving marriage and it's anything but bondage. I guess I look at the whole thing that way because of my circumstances. I guess you have other circumstances that truly color your view of love and relationships."

"The funniest thing," she now said, looking down at the floor for a moment, "is that my father thought it would be great for me to come here for this seminar because he claims that Judaism helps him live better. It's like if we cloak the topic of the day in religious rightness, it will all be okay."

"Is he abusing you?"

"Yes." Her eyes were now as dry as sand.

"What about your mother?"

"She left a long time ago. So now he picks on me."

"And you say that he tries to rationalize his behavior by referring to his religion?" I was curious.

"I don't know exactly. He just thinks that if I hang around a temple—even for a seminar on abuse—it will somehow make everything all right. He's sick."

"Saying that is probably your first step in dealing with this. Now, it's time for us to stop what we were doing until a few minutes ago: Talking in circles. I want to help you. I know that you want to be helped. You are not alone. For that matter, neither is your dad. This whole thing is not about hymens or fallen temples or wedding ceremonies.

It's about you and your right not to live in fear. Will you trust me?"

"I'll try," said the eighteen year old who finally let the terrified child in her come out from behind her eyes.

It would be several months later, after Saralyce had undergone productive personal and group therapy, and after her father had submitted to a county-operated community health program for sex offenders, that the young woman and I spoke some more about spiritual issues. She had embraced the redeeming notion of a local abuse prevention center that victims can become survivors. A series of clinical interviews and a comprehensive study of three generations in her family history revealed a successive pattern of intrafamily abuse. Now, Saralyce, brimming with hope and still strong-willed, wanted me to give her some Jewish insight about the problem of abuse.

"Saralyce, I want to tell you about something. I don't pretend to be able to respond to your experience and to your past hurt and anger all in one swoop, but I want to share something. I am thinking about a young woman, a prisoner of war actually, being held by her captors, who might very well be planning to abuse her."

"What are you talking about?!" I was so relieved to note that the darkness, the edginess of our original meeting were considerably lifted. She was smiling and intrigued.

"Well, I am talking about a woman I read about in the Bible. I am talking about a woman who wants to trim her fingernails, wash her face, and comb her hair.

"Who is this person?" Saralyce's eyes were quiet and deep.

"She does not have a name, but she is identified in the Bible as any potential female prisoner taken in battle by the Hebrews. You see, when the Hebrews were about to come into their promised land, it was understood that they would have to wage some battles in order to acquire the land. That was the reality in the same way that all of our lives invariably involve some battles. Anyway, Moses transmits some rules to his people. It's right there in the Bible."

"This is something I'm sure I never heard about when my parents dragged me to Hebrew school," interrupted Saralyce. "But what about this woman who wants to wash her face?"

"The point is that if a woman is captured, the soldiers have to at least show some restraint and compassion before taking her away. This is included in the ancient rules of war of the Jewish people. The men have to give her privacy and allow her to wash her face, trim her fingernails, and put herself together. They have to give her time so that she can take care of her hair. They have to allow her a chance to regain her sense of dignity and worth at the very time she feels potentially most violated. This is what the Hebrews are told they have to do."

"In a war?"

"That's the whole point. War is the worst thing that people do as a group. War, even when it's necessary, smothers every good human instinct. It makes men into butchers and, quite often, women into victims. Yet it's at this most inhumane of times that the biblical tradition tries to remind people to be humane. Before the soldiers might abuse their female captive, they have to allow her some quiet moments of composure. It's a hedge against what they might be inclined to do, in the hope that they will even refrain completely from doing her harm. It's a reminder that every person is a human being, regardless of the circumstances."

"But the wars still happened, didn't they?"

"Wars still happened then and they still do now. Same for family violence, and certainly, as you know so well, the same for abuse—of all kinds. Maybe you've learned in your hard work at the clinic, and maybe your father has begun to understand, that you simply can't extract the evil impulse from a human being. We all have a mixture of good and evil in us; it doesn't fly in from the outside. We all struggle with it. Some of us are better than others at containing it. Some of us abuse others, even our own children, because of something that a parent did to us. I'm just trying to tell you that, as far back as the Bible, people were asked—at their worst moments—to draw a breath, to contain the impulse, to hold their hands back. Sometimes it worked, sometimes it didn't. But one thing your father miscalculated while he was hurting you was that his religion in any way rationalized or condoned his behavior."

Saralyce looked up at me. "Maybe my religion will someday help me to be able to forgive him. But not yet, Rabbi. Do you think it will ever be possible?"

"Maybe—when you are lucky enough to find someone with whom to really share love. That's what your father denied you in his misguided behavior. He took away your ability to know and give love—for a while. He made you similar to that woman prisoner in the Bible."

"Thank you, Rabbi," said Saralyce. "I suddenly want to go and wash my face."

Naturally, I think about Saralyce whenever the question of abuse comes up in my work. What concerns me is that most young people who are mentally, physically, or sexually abused at home are not likely to be as outspoken as Saralyce. Moreover, the victims of abuse are not always in their teens; small children who suffer in this way are only able to feel terror and have little recourse to communicate the situation but for their obvious bruises.

A friend of mine, a pediatrician, sees or senses these bruises in many young people. "The parents will come into the hospital," says Brian, "and act like the bloody face or the broken arm was some kind of accident. And yet, they are often clearly remorseful, and it doesn't take much for them to admit or concede that they have beaten up their kid."

"Why do they do it?" I ask Brian.

"Really, so often because it was done to them. It's really a kind of disease. People need to recognize their capacity to do it and to acknowledge that they have it in them."

The numbers are worrisome. The Children's Defense Fund asserts that every single day in America over seven thousand children are reported abused or neglected. The CDF also finds that every day in this country three children die from abuse. No ethnic group or economic segment of our society is immune in a land so wealthy yet so poor that, every day, 100 babies die before their first birthday and 100,000 children remain homeless. We are apt to separate ourselves from this reality even though every one of us, by virtue of being human, is potentially capable of abusing another person—even our own children.

Am I suggesting that most people abuse their children? Absolutely not! What I am suggesting has to do with what my tradition has taught me about human nature: It's complicated and changeable. There isn't a good parent alive who can deny that he or she—at some trying moment—could have struck a child. Violence exists in the world because people exist in it. It doesn't come from the heavens; it comes from a darker side of the human soul. The Bible certainly has no illusions about what family members can and will do to each other; Genesis has barely unfolded before Cain slays his brother Abel. I think that when a teenager asks a parent about abuse, a parent has to start with the acknowledgement that human beings all have the capacity to hurt each other and that, tragically, some parents are simply unable to control the impulse. Blaming family violence or family abuse upon some satanic force or an external curse is a rationalization that places the responsibility for healthy family relations somewhere outside the house. We can certainly agree that abuse is evil, but, as I asserted in chapter five, we just can't place evil anywhere else but in human hands.

No scientific report I have examined has ever implicated a celestial force in the matter of family abuse. On the other hand, most religious traditions agree with the Talmudic plea for the sanctity of a human being: "Why was humanity created with the making of a single person?" This question is posed in the rabbinic literature. After all, it is true: God made people by starting with one individual. "To teach," comes the reply, "that if you destroy one life, it is as if you have destroyed the entire world, and if you save one life, it is as though you have saved the entire world."

The Bible tells of a place called Gilead, where an outbreak of civil disorder occurred. Everybody was fighting with everybody else; anger and rancor filled the streets of the province. As the French have said, the more things change, the more they stay the same; you can draw a straight line from Gilead of old to virtually any American city of today. Meanwhile, the rabbinic literature tried to analyze the urban violence exemplified by Gilead. The rabbis answered the question of why the violence occurred: "Because they made what is primary secondary and what is secondary primary." How so? "Because they loved their possessions more than their own children."

Many parents have possessions—cars, calculators, computers, coffeemakers, credit cards, and contact lenses. We're often in a hurry; we live apart from our children who carry on in their own well-endowed bedroom cubicles replete with phones, disc players, and electronic terminals. Unfortunately, it's easy to come across our children once in a while, on the way up and down the stairs, on the way out the door for the car pool, and suddenly feel as though these little people are strangers. This unsettling realization does not mean that we are going to abuse anybody. But that first layer of a human fault line—neglect—may be settling in. Ultimately, it's much harder to harm a child you really understand than a child who has become like so many other disposable objects that happen to be in your home. Most parents love their children; a lot of parents don't know their children.

Meanwhile, the term *abuse*—like many other words

and phrases—has become something of a buzzword in the very chatty 1990s. It seems to be an almost required revelation in the biographies of famous television and movie stars. I do not wish to take away from the courage of some of these renowned talk-show guests, but I would like to take away from the emotional inflation of the word *abuse*. When a teenager asks about abuse, he or she may be raising the subject because of the suspicion that a friend or classmate is suffering in some way.

That other youngster may indeed be in trouble. We are all responsible for one another. A discreet inquiry, perhaps involving professional people, may be in order. But it's important to clarify what a teenager is talking about when he or she suggests "abuse." The denial of telephone rights or the use of the car do not necessarily constitute abuse. And when your son or daughter says that you are "abusing" him or her because you are restricting that child to the house for some disciplinary reason, you need to have an open and genuine discussion of the meaning and implications of the term *abuse*.

Another wonderful physician I know tells me that she left the area of child abuse a few years ago "because of all the vigilantism." In today's kinetic culture, we are all so busy checking each other, suing each other, correcting each other, that a nursery school teacher who hugs or kisses a child is suddenly a potential suspect. Yes, there are some unhealthy people who staff day care centers and there are certainly some sick teachers, counselors, and clergy who are guilty of some serious crimes. But society itself is sick when a loving embrace or a supportive stroke of the hair is potentially a legal discussion when it is usually just an act of kindness. Everybody needs to calm down just as sure as those who are in fact abusive need to be stopped and rehabilitated.

A long time ago, an unlucky woman surrounded by angry men was given the chance to wash her face. It may have saved her from a cruel fate. Today we have so many children, including the ones in our own homes, whose faces we should be studying very carefully. There is much they fear and too much that they know. It wouldn't hurt to go talk to your child and spend some time washing faces together and, in the interim, cleansing souls.

CHAPTER 17

Why Doesn't God
Talk to Me?

It was a seventeen year old, Melanie, who asked me this question directly. She felt that she had good reason: Her aunt, a successful young businesswoman, had recently killed herself. Melanie was among those who discovered her aunt's body under a snowy tree along the banks of a frozen local creek. Melanie's grandfather, a beloved local physician who never had too much money because he didn't always believe in imposing upon his patients with bills, died from depression a few months later. Melanie's lonely aunt had been the doctor's daughter. Now, Melanie, her lips streaked with a vivid magenta lipstick and her eyes obscured by heavy shadow, sat in my study.

"Why doesn't God talk to me?"

"Have you tried to talk to God?" I inquired.

"Yes, but I feel no response. No, that's not true," added

the young girl. She was sad and withdrawn; I could barely hear her even though she sat across from me in my study. "No, it's not true that I feel no response. No. The response is an evil force that kills people I love."

"Do you think that God is responsible for that?"

"Hardly. God isn't involved. God won't even talk to me." I remember thinking that Melanie spoke as though she was under a spell of some kind. What a fallen child! She was denying God and decrying God in the same cold breath. But then, she stunned me with her next slow and measured statement:

"You know, I've been exploring some witchcraft."

"Tell me more," I said, clearing my throat.

Becoming more animated, Melanie proceeded to tell me about her need to meet the obvious evil in her life head-on. After her grandfather's death, she told me, she took a journey to New Zealand with a friend of hers who already had associations with witches. There, they studied the rites and customs of the Maori peoples, who believe in cosmic sorcery and in the wisdom of murky forces. "You've got to get control of the force," Melanie told me in a quiet but firm voice. She was contemplating another field trip— this time to New Mexico, where she could link up with the wizardry of Hopi Indians. "Maybe if I had known something about these forces before, I could have prevented the madness from consuming and killing my aunt," she told me. She described for me the "devil's marks" she saw on her aunt's body when she and the police made the terrible discovery. Others had pleaded with her that these were just birthmarks but she did not recall noticing the patches while her aunt was still alive. I felt my heart breaking into so many pieces inside of me, even as I understood that I had never been with a young person so desperately in need of the very God she was denying with her reservoir of potions, magic words, and dark enchantments.

I asked Melanie: "Do you want to talk to me about the witchcraft or do you want to talk about God?"

"Well, why doesn't God talk to me?"

"God doesn't actually talk to anybody," I answered, "in the way that your experiences in witchcraft would perhaps lead you to expect a conversation." I waited a moment for a reaction. Her face was blank, so I proceeded:

"A wizard can give you a quick answer, Melanie, and I suppose that I understand that you might want that sometimes. You and your family have suffered a lot of loss." I spoke from experience; I had officiated at the funerals of both of the girl's relatives. Her aunt, although outwardly felicitous, was actually an unhappy and unlucky person. Her heart had been broken in several categories. Melanie's grandfather had truly been a saint who rewarded his many patients with uncommon personal care and an abiding commitment to medicine more as a science than an enterprise. I myself have wondered why fate would have been so unkind to a man who was such a healer and public servant.

But God is not directly responsible for these things, I tried to explain to the troubled girl in my office. My tradition does not expect that from heaven. Real life happens on the earth. It would be a heavy burden on the human race to expect God to account for this cancer cell or that maladaptive brain wave. God is neither a chemist nor a psychiatrist and God is certainly not a wizard. If human beings were to truly hold God immediately liable for every twist of fate, then how could we possibly account for the world described in this morning's newspaper?

Every youngster feels, from time to time, that God is not communicating. Every youngster occasionally turns to some form of "witchcraft" (although I consider a diversion such as Melanie's to be extremely dangerous and such a person in need of healthy intervention). Again, as my tradition has declared: "The world is too much with us." Sickness and death can overwhelm the human spirit, and when the world around us seems more than can we bear, God serves a purpose by being the one we can deny, reject, or blame.

When my own father died suddenly many years ago, I told my rabbi that God hadn't heard my prayers. My father had shown signs of stress and discontent for a few years; his sudden heart attack was exactly what I feared would happen. I had even dreamed of his death. Now I felt that God had failed to communicate with me. I was very angry at God.

The rabbi told me: "That's fine. Be angry at God. God can take it. Better that than you should be angry at yourself or your mother or somebody else over your father's death. None of us could take that kind of anger. God can absorb it."

I probably was already figuring out then, even in my grief, that God was not responsible for the myocardial infarction that killed my father. A combination of poor spiritual health and vascular problems were what caused it. So, I came to understand, God did not decree that this premature death should occur. Rather, God would be the source for me to draw strength from in dealing with this reality. This is the essential dynamic we must convey to our children when the world caves in and they start to indict the heavens: God doesn't make people sick, God does not make people kill each other, God does not start wars. But God is the starting point for healing and, quite often, the inspiration for somebody to do something in order to calm a soul specifically or to repair the world generally.

A parent may ask, why does my child expect God to listen and talk? In the first place, a young person does this because we fill children with that hope when they are very young. Secondly, it's a healthy and natural yearning for anybody to want God to know what's inside the heart. Thirdly, teenagers are getting quick answers and problem resolutions from a number of modern sources that require no spiritual recourse and yield no pain. Teenagers listen to voice mail, video games, and a number of interactive communicative sources that retrieve and share the information instantly. They interact with cybernetic, self-serve fuel pumps and automated bank tellers that talk to them and complete equations. They are more in touch with fiber optics than they are with real eyes and ears. It's easy for a teenager to exist today; it's not so easy to *live*!

Sometimes, when emotional and spiritual accounts become tangled, kids wonder why God, like some kind of divine cash machine, doesn't seem to emerge with a prompt answer. All of this is a product of today's convenient living, but it becomes very inconvenient when your child is really confused or even broken in spirit. There is a lot a parent can and should do to make sure that a child feels like somebody is communicating. The fact is that God talks to people—through other people.

"Why doesn't God respond to my pain?" Melanie wanted to know. She clearly expected some distinct and evident voice from above, but no religion can effectively guarantee such an expectation or promise. That kind of drama is better confined to the world of television evangelists, where a combination of dollars and Nielsen ratings yield short-term redemption for many and long-term cash flow for a very few.

The fact is that God's presence in human life is not so audible. It is subtle, mysterious, and more generally detected between human spirits. The only person in the Hebrew Scripture who actually spoke directly with God—"face to face"—was Moses. Time and time again, a section of the biblical story begins with the phrase: "And the Lord spoke to Moses, saying . . ." Everybody else, from Abraham to Rebekah to Joshua to Deborah, sensed or believed or *felt* what God was telling them. The communication came in dreams, through angels, or in moments of either stress or inspiration. The correspondence between God and people is not so much loud incantation as it is quiet poetry. It is much more efflorescent than it is crystalline; real breakthroughs occur more often in a corner of the human soul than across a mountaintop.

Moses was truly an exception. Believing as I do that the Bible is, in so many ways, telling the story of democracy, I wonder sometimes why Moses had this remarkable privilege. He and God actually chatted. The rest of us discover God in our visions, our reveries, and certainly in our prayers. So why did God talk to Moses? I think that in order to tell heaven's story to the earth, God had to speak with one special person who would, in turn, convey the message to other people. So ultimately God's voice is heard when people mouth the words among one another. In spite of his divine conversations, Moses still seems motivated to do heavenly things because of his interaction with other persons. Pharaoh's slave-talk offends him, the crying of the Hebrews moves him, the comforting words of his wife and his father-in-law (as we noted in chapter fifteen) reassure him. I think that God talked directly to Moses because Moses was exemplary in the category of listening to other human voices.

An older gentleman came to see me one day. Like Melanie, this individual had suffered an inordinate amount of loss in his family. I certainly understood and sympathized when he asked me: "Where is the hand of God for me?" He then proceeded to describe the unyielding fealty of his sister, who looked after him, who accompanied him to the grocery store, who had assisted him with the painful task of selecting his wife's tombstone, who helped him pay his bills, and who had just driven him to the temple for this appointment. "Look at your sister's hands, Mr. Eckerstein. Don't you see God's palm working?"

Of course, not everybody who has suffered is so fortunate to have other hands and other voices convey God's messages. When Melanie came to see me about her loneliness, I wondered to myself about her parents. They had urged her to visit with me, but I did not, frankly, get the feeling that they had spoken much with her about the troubles they all shared. There is a tendency towards stoicism in some families that sometimes leaves people beyond each other's reach. Melanie's parents were also grieving for two people in their family, but in a sense they were allowing death to take away more than it was entitled to take. A child dabbling in witchcraft, having an inaccessible God to suspect, is a child who needs to hear soothing voices at home. I think that our children would hear God's voice more often if only parents would form the words.

If we want our youngsters to believe that God will speak with and listen to them, then we must create the atmosphere of dialogue around the breakfast table, in the backyard, along the bedside. In such a discordant world, I certainly believe it is healthy for any young person to feel or know some intimacy with his or her God. I remember how touched I was one night when my younger daughter, Debra, told me that she cherishes her talks with God. I felt good about it because I know that Cathy and I have not promised Debra or Sari any immediate miracles from God, nor any prizes or rewards save for the inner satisfaction of such conversation. Since *we* all talk to each other, it is normal for my daughter to feel that God is also talking.

"It feels better talking with God," Debra told me, "than even writing in my diary. What I write in my diary is actually just for me, and no one else is supposed to know what I've put down. That's okay, but when I talk to God, wherever I am, I really know that someone is listening."

I once asked several members of my Confirmation class at the temple to write down some of their thoughts about God. Predictably, a diverse and fascinating body of answers and ruminations was produced. The responses ranged from

"I doubt God" to "He only loves" to "we are all God." One youngster wrote that "God isn't real because people die young and the wars and things like that . . ." Another wrote: "I think God is a belief to turn to when I need to talk to someone or have something to turn to that will listen."

On paper, these youngsters' notes combined into a kind of generic diary of human yearnings about God. But I knew the children who made these notes that day and could discern a relationship between their assertions about God and their personal lives. I had no problem, as such, with those who "doubt" God; my sadness came when I read about anger, bitterness, and loneliness. What they decried about God often betrayed a situation at home. Children who were obviously being heard at home tended to verify their belief in themselves by their thoughtful and open discourse concerning God, pro or con!

One evening at home, I was feeling sorry for myself. Things were not going so well in my work; I was uncertain about some things and despondent in general. For several days, I hadn't let anybody in my family really help me. Then, Debra came into the room, smiling and excited. She had just returned from a brief shopping excursion with Cathy. "Dad, guess what we saw?"

In a pool of self-pity, I hardly responded. My daughter continued: "You should have seen it! It was a rainbow in the sky, a double rainbow! Oh, it was so beautiful. All of a sudden, there it was—a rainbow!"

I looked up, as Debra's excited words broke through my loneliness with light, color, and hope. I realized that God was speaking to me through my child. When does God talk to us? When another person comes along to make the sound.

CHAPTER 18

༄༅

Is It Okay for Me
to Say What I Think?

Looking at the social landscape of our country, it could be argued that, in some ways, we and our children have been living in the civilization of Roseanne. The notorious television actress and outrageous personage, by virtue of her outlandish public statements and uninhibited outbursts, is a kind of personification of the era. Whether blaspheming the national anthem at a baseball game or spreading her bile against her former husband during a broadcast interview, Roseanne's singular contribution to American discourse can be summarized simply: It's too loud, too self-serving, too undisciplined, too much. Some may say that Roseanne is simply outspoken. I hope that most parents and teenagers would recognize that—in spite of her reasonably good sitcom about an American family— in real life, she's simply brazen.

The problem is that, to some degree, this kind of behavior has settled into mainstream standards. Loud talk is perceived as outspokenness when, in fact, a person should consider being outspoken based more upon strong convictions than on powerful lungs. Abraham Lincoln was outspoken too; his compelling messages about human dignity and the integrity of a nation still resonate across the years with a quiet authority. I suspect that Lincoln's kind of outspokenness will still reverberate long after the last shrill echo has subsided from the mouths of *People* magazine icons such as Roseanne, Andrew Dice Clay, or the last person who knew something revealing about the late Nicole Simpson.

There is a difference between speaking loudly and speaking out. In previous decades here in America, some people carried over the British tendency towards reticence. Truly, children were to be seen but not heard. Although this reluctance to acknowledge kids is still found in some households and some schools, our nation has matured in its appreciation of children's needs. We find in their voices, their humor, their curiosity, something refreshing and heartening. It is safe to say that most adults genuinely understand that a society's health can be measured by the general welfare and inner peace of its children.

Meanwhile, Roseanne notwithstanding, we do live in a country where people are encouraged to express themselves. Ethnic groups and other identifiable categories of people are urged to feel validated and to experience empowerment. People who have the same skin color, people who are left-handed, people who are physically challenged—all are roused, in one way or another, to convey their desire to be enabled. We have already discussed the latent negative effect of this trend: The election of one kind of person sometimes implies the rejection of another. Nevertheless, the issue being raised here is that, in the 1990s, parents are raising children in an environment that stresses personal or collective affirmation. Even children are considered to be a social grouping in need of protection, identification, and certain legal rights.

The point is that a lot of people are talking. They are being given, or they are seizing, platforms and soapboxes at public meetings, on call-in shows, and television segments. It sometimes feels like we are caught up in a national stir-fry of sizzling chatter. Some of it is interesting and even redeeming. A lot of it is self-serving or promotional. All of it adds up to a culture based largely upon the very right of people to make statements. So the next time you have the urge to tell your youngster to shut up, remember that he or she is coming of age in a civilization that is admonishing everyone to "get out there" and say what they feel.

And yet words have power. Words represent a certain literacy that often transcends the more nebulous realms of "communication" and "interactive programming." What people say to each other is really important—especially if the talk is grounded in sincerity, concern, or passion. We may wish to curtail our kids' loquaciousness from time to time, but doing so creates the risk that a young person will not say something significant and heartfelt. When a child is outspoken, he or she is not just verbalizing a matter of personal consequence. The youngster is also taking chances, testing the waters of a relationship and, in a real sense, drawing away the curtains from the window of the inner self. Being outspoken may be dismissed as rudeness, and it may indeed be indulgent. But we should listen; some truths may be heard. And if we truly surmise that what we are hearing is just an outburst, then we as adults have the responsibility of clarifying what is speech and what is just verbiage.

Not long after I became senior rabbi of my congregation at the tender age of thirty-seven, an older member took me out to lunch to talk things over. In his seventies, his view of me was somewhat analogous to that of a parent regarding his or her teenager. Sympathetic but critical, the gentleman commented that he was pleased with the suit I was wearing: "I like seeing my rabbi in pinstripes." In general, he told me, I shouldn't be "too loud." "Don't ever say too much," he cautioned. "People should see you in the room, but should always have to wonder a little bit what you are really thinking." In general, he summarized, the best thing for a young rabbi like me to do was to exhibit what he called "restrained leadership."

As with most things, I recognized some worthwhile advice in the gentleman's remarks, while filtering out some of the more gratuitous aspects. I was struck by the useful notion of "restrained leadership," and remember that phrase better than anything else in the lunchtime conversation. In general, I thought that my congregant was asking me to avoid making a lot of noise but he was not asking me to keep quiet, either. I think we need to find that kind of balance in dealing with our children's desires and needs to be heard. The fact is that our kids live in an extraordinarily competitive and clamorous society. It's not so easy to be heard even when others are willing to listen. We often encourage our children to be ambitious. Ambition will not be driven by complacency. The fact is that nobody ever got elected to anything, made it to outer space, won a peace prize, or appeared in a movie because he or she was completely passive. Now, most young people are not committed to nor will they realize such lofty situations, but they are certainly yearning to achieve some level of personal goals. If we don't look, listen, and love, we just might miss something worthwhile.

I know a teenager named Ted who loves to talk, who enjoys singing, going out with friends, and teasing the person next to him. Ted has unrepining spirits, a friendly smile, and a sharp tongue. He exhibits leadership around his school that is not yet necessarily restrained. But he really cares about the world around him, is loyal to his classmates, and is very capable of compassion and insight. In the past, when I've been with Ted and his family, his parents seemed embarrassed by his animated ways. They are fairly reserved people who have sometimes disclaimed their boisterous son: "Hard to believe he isn't adopted!"

There was a crisis in Ted's family. His father had gone into a business with poor backing and meager prospects. Ted's father, with a tendency towards brooding, had grown weary of answering to a boss. He had a private dream of financial and professional independence. That, combined with a resentment for authority, led him into a series of mistakes. The father's underlying reticence about things, and his evident air of frustration, have probably been factors in Ted's need to be declarative.

Ted's parents generally discouraged their son's high-flung personality. "Be quiet, Ted," they said several times when I joined them for dinner. "There's no need to comment about everything."

There came a need, however, for Ted to comment on something. His father was drifting away from the family (including two other, younger children). The father was spending longer hours at the failing business, struggling in vain to turn things around. He was drifting into depressed spirits. He was kicking his dead dream and, to some degree, turning his disappointment with life onto his children. Eventually, Ted decided it was time to speak out.

Ted intuitively knew that confronting his despondent dad would not be the most effective option. He sensed that his father was not a good listener. Ted wrote his dad a letter and left it on his father's forlorn desk at the business. I eventually learned about the contents of this note from Ted's father.

Ted told his dad that he was worried about him. He wrote that the family no longer had dinner together very often, and that all five members of the household were in a different orbit. They needed their leader back. "Come home to us, Daddy," wrote the son. Ted told his father in this note that they all understood his disappointment in the business. They all recognized the father's aversion to "being bossed around by somebody else." But the family could make up in love whatever their father might have to put up with in a regular job. Ted understood that his father wanted more security. "But the dollars just aren't worth the value of our family, Daddy."

Ted's father keeps his son's note in a special place. He no longer is apologetic for Ted's outgoing demeanor. He no longer pleads with his son to be silent. The father has adjusted to a new job situation, and he has adjusted even better to his son's outspokenness.

Words are potentially powerful instruments that can change lives. I remember learning about this in the mid-1970s, when it was briefly my responsibility to serve as a visiting student rabbi in Jasper, Alabama. Jasper was a sleepy, bourbon-soaked town of magnolias, camellias, and pines set about thirty-five miles northwest of Birmingham. One of its key claims to fame is the house where its famous denizen, Tallulah Bankhead, had lived. I conducted religious services in this town at the ancient and declining Temple Emanuel, a synagogue set stoically on a street corner adjacent to three formidable churches. The one religion, however, that transcended all others in this corner of the world was college football—especially on those Saturdays when Alabama played Auburn. I firmly believed that this regional pigskin ritual had more to do with God than whatever any of us four clergymen could possibly say at that ecumenical street corner in Jasper.

My visits to Jasper occurred some six years before George Wallace's fourth and final election as governor of the state. Birmingham, where my plane landed once a month, was already on its way to the post–Jim Crow era of modernization and renewal, but it still wasn't until 1979 that a black was elected mayor of what had been known as the "Johannesburg of America." This city of steel, now fast becoming the "Pittsburgh of the South," nevertheless clung to some of its obdurate social thinking in the mid-1970s. I sensed it, and somewhat feared it, even as my visits seemed safe and sanitary and were replete with the normal and strangely reassuring franchise symbols of Thrifty Rent-A-Car, Holiday Inn, and other cookie-cutter logos that were finally blurring the difference between Birmingham and Pittsburgh.

So it was a time of transition. On the surface, Jasper looked like everywhere else in America, but the plantation mentality still fluttered through the blossom-scented trees of US 78 and Route 5. Here, where these two roads intersected, even Jewish people ate grits for breakfast, sounded like Robert E. Lee, and listened to me trying to scratch out a sermon on certain Friday evenings.

During the course of one of my visits, I had occasion to talk with a small group of local men who were also enjoying breakfast at the motel restaurant. They were friendly enough and I struck up a conversation. They appeared to be in their forties and fifties and would surely have a clear memory of the recent era of civil rights confrontations in their state. One of the men had been expounding on the positive benefits experienced in his hometown of Tuscumbia—where the federally mandated Tennessee Valley Authority created cheap and plentiful industrial power. "Things had to change down here," he mused in a long drawl. "After all, we eventually got Goodyear and Ford, and we all finally started to earn a living." Another member of the group—which graciously included me in the breakfast conversation—celebrated the impact of NASA and Pentagon monies on Huntsville, the site of the Marshall Space Flight Center. Of course, these reports of some prosperity in certain Alabama communities belied the immense poverty of much of the state, especially where black families were and are concentrated.

Nevertheless, the discourse was inviting and cordial, so I decided to put forth a question. I offered that I was truly fascinated by the evident change in social attitudes that were also now part of Alabama. The already crippled but still feisty George Wallace was gearing up for another run for the White House (he would be preempted by a neighboring Southern governor, Jimmy Carter), but even Wallace —perhaps tempered by his bullet wounds—was ostensibly moderated in his views. "What really happened down here to make folks change a bit in their view of black people and the way people generally should live together?"

One of the men proceeded to candidly tell me that he had been a personal friend and admirer of Eugene "Bull" Connor, the malevolent Birmingham police chief who turned the fire hoses and the dogs on black demonstrators before news cameras in the 1960s. "Yeah, but things have changed," he shrugged.

"Well, what was it that made it change? Was it the news media that forced people to think it over?"

"Yeah, I suppose," said the same man. "But you know, it was really something else. In those days, we heard a lot of people saying a lot of things. King came around once in a while—I remember when he sat in the Birmingham jail and wrote that letter to the other ministers in town. A few of us heard him talk." The others assented.

"Well, to tell you the truth, it wasn't so much what the government was forcing on us or what the new laws were turning out to be. That was part of it, but not all of it. A few of us heard Reverend King. And, actually, it was what he was saying that made a difference to some of us. It was just those words of his. He talked, and most people up north just figured that no one heard anything he was saying down here. He was one outspoken preacher, I'll say that. It was his words that got to us, mostly."

Dr. Martin Luther King, Jr. was, to say the least, an outspoken man. America often makes outspoken men and women (including Abraham Lincoln) pay dearly for their convictions. But I was moved to hear a group of unlikely Southern workers concede that his words were powerful enough to help them look at life differently. I think it's a good reminder to be careful before we curtail the spirit and the voice of any youngster with something on his mind. Speaking out certainly made it possible for a youngster named Ted to help restore his family, even as one brave preacher's words did something for the soul of a nation. Is it okay for me to say what I think? In other words, how far should outspokenness go? It should go exactly as far as the distance between a person's mouth and that same person's heart.

CHAPTER 19

Why Are Celebrities Looked Up to, Even When They Send Out the Wrong Messages?

When I was growing up in the 1950s and 1960s, celebrities were essentially celebrities. Distant from us, conveyed normally in grainy, black-and-white television images, unavailable via a direct call-in show hookup, these people were easy to deify. We had no particular reason not to believe in them and we certainly had little information with which to indict them. But although they may have appeared pristine, it turns out that some of those people, such as Marilyn Monroe, Jayne Mansfield, and Elvis Presley, were not so perfect and could have used some more information themselves. They did not always respect themselves, they were sometimes abusive of their bodies, and they were often not very heroic.

We really did not know too much about them. That was part of their mystique. If rock stars were indulging in tranquilizers, it was not always part of our storehouse of knowledge. If baseball players were gambling, we were not sharing in the risk. If aspiring presidents were womanizing, we were not aware of it and, therefore, our view of such public people remained focused more on the issues of leadership than on libido. It was easier to have heroes then to the same extent that it was easier to be deceived.

Do young people have heroes today? They do, but their heroes are more human, even as young people are understandably more cynical. In a sense, they have less to lose; our generation still mourns the loss of its assassinated heroes because these men died in more or less a state of public innocence. All we knew, for example, was that President Kennedy was young, lithe, brilliant. We have trouble embracing the revelations that came later about his personal habits and his weaknesses. We don't want dark clouds to obscure the blue skies of our hero-worship.

But we have to put the issues of celebrity and idolatry in perspective. There was talent a generation ago, and there is certainly talent now. Without question, teenagers have people worth admiring today in a number of categories. In fact, it can be argued that there is greater skill out there than ever before. Runners go faster than before, musicians play more instruments and tour much harder than before, artists engage more mediums, stage performers are more athletic, and athletes more charismatic than before. It is important to consider the quality of talent even if we cannot always revere the quality of those who are talented.

Meanwhile, it is not so good for young people to unquestioningly venerate anybody in the public domain. They are likely to be disappointed, even as so many celebrities, including ice-skaters, congressmen, and pop singers have disappointed us. Judaism has something to say about this in the way that it regards, for example, the story of Noah.

Most people know the saga of Noah and the ark. It is an enduring children's story because of the charming notion of all the animals marching, two by two, from the dry land into the big boat. But this account is at the surface of the story. A layer or two deeper is the question of evil and corruption and of just how wonderful Noah, the man, really was or wasn't.

There were clearly no heroic role models in the days that preceded the terrible flood. The Bible indicates that God was completely disheartened by the collective behavior of God's human experiment. "The whole earth was corrupt," the text says. It's actually a bitter tale about a very angry God who essentially drowns the entire human race. God decides to spare the remnants of life, however. That is why God picks one individual to build this ark and collect two of every kind of species. God is disappointed in humankind, but wants to start over nonetheless.

We really don't know why this fellow Noah is the one who is spared and is given the responsibility of the ark. There is no indication in the text of his renown, of any particular celebrity status or war medals or community awards. He is neither an elected official nor a talk show host nor a best-selling author. The Bible just says that "Noah was a righteous man in his times." From this, one can derive that he had some kind of superior moral quality and therefore stood out.

But just how superior was Noah? Should he be automatically extolled? Just how great was he? The Bible seems to qualify Noah's exalted status. The Bible does not assert that Noah was simply "a righteous man." The text indicates that he was righteous *"in his times."* Since the times in question were the worst ever known—so tawdry that God felt compelled to wipe humanity out—just how good did that make Noah?

Everything, including celebrity, is relative. The true nobility of a person, whether he or she is well-known or not, is based upon a combination of personal integrity and the need for that person's talents at that particular time. In a better age, Noah may not have been so notable. But the Bible makes a cogent point when it suggests that "greatness" depends, to some degree, upon when and where a person lives.

I think that celebrities today are sending out "the wrong messages" because our society does not have a built-in expectation that famous people are supposed to send out "right messages." The moral value of any message being transmitted by a celebrity is too often distilled by a frenetic media before it can be discerned in a classroom or around the living room at home. We parents and teachers are bushwhacked by the amoral commentators of productions such as *A Current Affair* and *Inside Edition*. The growing cooperation of traditional news programs in the syndicating of information adds to the moral fuzz that attends public people. Kids are getting the wrong messages because a large media are depending upon these messages for the accumulation of ratings. The result is a culture that has reduced the ethical language between the public and private domains to a series of bizarre reports about this one's sex life and that one's burst of violence.

Whether they are crime suspects (like O.J. Simpson), Olympic victims or coconspirators (like Nancy Kerrigan and Tonya Harding), movie stars or ballplayers, we have to remember that the people we adulate or fawn over are celebrities in *these* times. If we as a civilization were not already so obsessed with sexual conduct, Michael Jackson's alleged behavior with young boys might not have been found so interesting. If we were not such a strident sports culture, the baseball and hockey players and owners who shut down their leagues in the mid-1990s would not have been so worthy of our disgust and condemnation. Indeed, it is the culture that defines a celebrity, not the other way around.

We don't demand the right things from our public figures, who therefore don't always send out the right messages to our kids. I thought this problem was clearly exemplified just a few years ago in Chicago, although the pattern I wish to illustrate is constant in our society. It came home to me during a radio newscast describing two separate incidents that seemed inexorably and sadly linked to one another.

It was announced that the Chicago city schools would be forced to drop athletics from their schedule because of budgetary problems. This kind of thing has become endemic in America, and it is as heartbreaking as it is telling. In Chicago, a somber committee of school principals came to the conclusion that the district would not have the 1.5 million dollars necessary to retain an after-school sports program. Then it was a second bit of news, heard during the same broadcast, that raised my levels of ire and concern even higher.

It turns out that on the same day that the principals anguished in Chicago, a professional football player named Webster Slaughter signed a 2.2 million-dollar contract to catch passes for the Houston Oilers. Slaughter, who did not invent the free-agent system but who certainly personifies it, was understandably delighted. True, he had already been receiving a hefty salary from the Cleveland Browns, but now a legal maneuver permitted him to walk out of Cleveland and get more dollars in Houston.

I thought: Lucky for Webster that he wasn't still just dreaming about playing pro football while going to high school in Chicago—or any other American city that can't raise enough cash to help boys and girls suit up with their hopes. He would have a hard time gaining celebrity or free-agent status without having played and been coached back on the varsity squad that wasn't.

Webster Slaughter and his many colleagues in several sports are not themselves the problems. But the system we all have agreed to, and the complicity of so many greedy athletes and their lawyers, agents, and fans is certainly a problem for young people all over this country.

It is hard for anyone working in a field such as mine—dealing with young souls in a turbulent civilization—to rationalize that an entire generation of deserving and talented kids won't be able to play football, baseball, or tennis on school fields and in gymnasiums while a handful of indulgent superstars will continue to impose their will on both our economic and social systems.

It's a question, again, of values. What I effectively heard in that newscast is that one individual is going to earn more in two years to play football than it would take to pay for an entire city school class to learn the game. There is more of a sanction to celebrity than to growth. This tells me a great deal about our nation, and is more informative than the series of gratuitous pronouncements about family values we've been hearing from our politicians over the past several years. This irony, that a sports personality can earn several times what it costs to create new sports talent and involved kids, is the bottom line on a society that suffers from a terrible deficit in social values. Such a system inevitably creates celebrities who sometimes lack an appreciation for genuine experience, and so you have the baseball player who throws a firecracker at fans, the heavyweight boxing champion who terrorizes women in hotels, the "brat" film star who can't control his pharmaceutical intakes or soundstage outbursts, the diva whose bad manners become too much even for her investors, the suburban, teenaged strumpet who was able to shoot, lure, and lie her way (with her unseemly adult accomplice and suitor) into no less than *three* prime-time melodramas—including two that were broadcast simultaneously! From Vince Coleman to Johnny Depp to Mike Tyson to Kathleen Battle to Amy Fisher, who can be surprised that some young people are complaining that today's "heroes" are a bit less than heroic?

We have to turn our children's attention away from the public domains of kitsch and selfishness and towards the more private domains of caring and service. I see heroes every day; they are not the subjects of commercial profiles. If your son or daughter were to spend any time watching people who heal wounds in a hospital, who prepare hot meals for cold stomachs in countless hunger centers, who play a little basketball after school with restless kids who might have been otherwise enlisted by gangs, who comfort the unwell and depressed in nursing homes—then your child might better understand what heroism really is. Even better, if a youngster participates, with your example, in acts that repair the world and heal souls, that youngster will not be so eager to believe in the celebrity of the celebrated. And, ultimately, the best magnate for a teenager rests in the quiet magnetism of a parent who knows his or her child well enough to share a skeptical laugh about the latest burst of indulgence that came through the television, the radio, or the sensation magazine.

Why are celebrities looked up to, even when they send out the wrong messages? The answer has a lot to do with the fact that, often enough, the wrong people are the celebrities.

CHAPTER 20

⚜

How Will I Know When
I Am Successful in Life?

There is an old saying in Judaism: "Shrouds have no pockets." It's a blunt phrase, based in common sense and reality. It refers to the burial shrouds that cover the dead. In contemporary terms, the rabbinic adage means simply, that when you die, you take nothing with you—not stocks, bonds, jewels, liquid assets, or lines of credit. Sometimes, when people become enthralled with the notion of material wealth and proceed to absolutely equate this with success, I am reminded of the brusque truth in what the rabbis expressed a long time ago.

It's not what you have, it's what you feel.

Considering the issues of money and celebrity that we have already examined, it's easy to see why young people sometimes get anxious about their capacities for success. While financial achievement is a worthy goal for anybody, it does not guarantee the ultimate success that there is in human life: Inner peace. As we learned with Noah, everything is relative. *Success* is perhaps the most subjective word in any language, except when it is applied to the one thing that everybody needs but nobody can buy—the quiet realization inside your gut that you are essentially happy and satisfied with your life.

If we want to help kids with this question, we might want to start by dispelling the notion that just because a person is in a lofty position, or in a seemingly enviable situation, that person is automatically successful and enviable. I want to share a story about a friend of mine named Jack.

Jack Aker is something of a legend in the world of professional baseball. I am a fan of the sport, and have been an admirer of its outstanding players and managers. One of the greatest and most enduring relief pitchers of all time, holder of the *Sporting News* Fireman of the Year Award in 1966, Jack played for the Kansas City and then Oakland Athletics, the Seattle Pilots, New York Yankees, Chicago Cubs, Atlanta Braves, and New York Mets. When I met Jack some years ago, he was the pitching coach of the Cleveland Indians; I caught my breath short, extending and receiving hands of friendship with a living and breathing major leaguer who was on first-name basis with such stars as Phil Niekro and Tom Seaver.

Jack had everything, I thought, including the ability to invite me for a private visit to the ballpark and clubhouse of an American League baseball club. There could be no success story greater than this.

I remember an occasion when Jack invited me to visit

the clubhouse and the dugout at the ballpark; it was very special for me, as it would be for any genuine follower of the sport. Arriving on the field before the game, Jack came for me, in full regalia—snappy cap and shimmering team jacket. He walked across fresh, chalky sidelines with a certain, lanky royalty. There was the first faint smell of popcorn from the bowels of the stadium as the coach escorted me to the clubhouse.

Jack took me into a comfortably large room filled with open booths that served as repositories for the players. "Here," he said, "we meet and discuss the game plan." The coach walked past the colognes and hair dryers of the bath toward a large bin containing polished baseball bats. "Nobody can touch a man's bat. You see, they are numbered according to his uniform number. The bat is a very personal matter to a guy. Nobody can touch it."

Nobody can touch you, Jack, I thought to myself in admiration and some awe.

Walking up a ramp, the infield grass came into my line of vision. I heard players limbering up on the diamond. As I walked up the steps to field level, I beheld a handful of the visitors at practice. The Indians manager watched them intently: He was like a general searching for clues to the weaknesses of the enemy. I thought to myself: Here, in the person of a major league manager, was the epitome of success.

I recalled the graceful tip of Jack's hat, the assertion of gentle power just a little over a year later, when Jack (and that same team manager, for that matter) were both summarily dismissed from their positions with the ball club. A disappointing record during the season of my clubhouse visit, and a subsequent poor start in the new season led to the successive firings. Now, this same Jack, my invincible hero, sat in the front seat of my automobile, shoulders slumped, his head in his hands. We were taking a drive in the country as the venerable coach tried to sort things out. His prestige, his income, and his self-image were suddenly as powdery as the faded chalk lines of that emerald ball field he had once ruled. Jack was gone, the manager was gone, as well as a number of the players I had gawked at that shining afternoon.

I tried to comfort Jack, a genuinely nice man who loves the game and who particularly loves to help younger ballplayers succeed. I found myself shaken; baseball was just another cruel enterprise, after all. Success was as fickle as the breeze coming across the pitcher's mound. Jack, like a piece of baseball tumbleweed, would bounce around for a little while longer as the pitching coach of a rudimentary minor league team in the Atlanta Braves system.

Jack is doing quite well now, a few years after his exit from the big leagues. He remembers his playing and coaching days fondly. He is surrounded by his very supportive wife, Jane, and their two sons. Jack has children and even grandchildren from previous marriages. His life is full with his extensive family circle. "I feel pretty good," he was able to tell me, acknowledging that his feelings of triumph are better grounded in love than in the grounds of a baseball stadium. In a way, Jack is truly and finally successful. *It's not what you have, it's what you feel.*

"My son has no ambition," a mother once told me. "He doesn't worry about adding up to anything because he knows that his father will take him into the business, provide everything he needs, buy him a house, and set up trust funds for his future. My son doesn't even wonder how to be successful, because it's all worked out for him already."

The teenager in question, Ryan, was really not such a bad sort. His mother was genuinely frustrated about what was basically Ryan's laziness. She may have also been lamenting her husband's well-intended, but not necessarily helpful habits of making everything perfect for Ryan and his younger sister.

I asked Ryan how he felt about his situation. "Lucky, I guess," he replied, rather lamely. He didn't sound too lucky to me, although he was clearly living in good fortune. I do meet a lot of young people who "have everything" but display a limited amount of insight on the meaning of success. Some of these teenagers are restless; they have a lot of time on their hands, and not too much creative tension to motivate or inspire them. They do not tend, for example, to be good readers or active writers or aficionados of anything or anyone in particular. They don't often attempt to present something at a science fair, or develop an interesting correspondence with someone noteworthy or worth emulating. Ryan, for example, admitted to me that he was just plain bored with life. He had too much, and he yearned for too little.

But he is a sweet young man, and he is blessed with a mother who wants him to aspire for more than just the material things he has. She asked me to "put a fire in him," so Ryan and I met in my study.

"What do you feel about the life you lead?" I asked Ryan.

"My father says I'm a success. He wants me to know that I will always have everything I can imagine."

"Well, what do you imagine?"

"I don't know. More of the same, I guess." Ryan looked uncomfortable. He stared at me, probably wondering what I wanted from him. Then he said: "I'm hungry."

"Terrific. Let's go get a snack. But let me ask you something, Ryan. Do you know what being hungry means?"

"Wanting something to eat, I guess."

"Yes, that's true," I answered. "But you know, Ryan, there are different meanings for that word. For you and me, and most of the people we know, thank goodness, hungry means we're ready for our next meal. But for a lot of people in our own city, hunger means they're going to die."

"What are you talking about?" The teenager was genuinely perplexed. We talked for a few moments about the problems of malnutrition and poverty that deprive many lives in America. Ryan seemed to have no idea. "Your father," I continued, "gives a lot of money regularly to the hunger fund in our temple. He's really very generous. I wonder if you'd like to see exactly what these donations do for people. I wonder if you'd like to feel something special inside of you by doing something that actually can't be measured in dollars."

Ryan was intrigued. We shared a snack and I invited him to join me and several members of our temple youth group for an outing that would occur two weeks later. The youngsters were going to visit a church near downtown Cleveland and prepare a meal for some two hundred nearby residents who depended on such acts of kindness in order to actually survive.

Ryan appeared at the temple on the day of the outing. His mother drove him over in the family van and immediately offered to join us in transporting youth group members who came out to fulfill this very good deed.

At the church, Ryan was transformed. He scrubbed pots and pans, set out paper tablecloths on the long picnic-style tables, and laid out endless sets of plastic silverware. He stirred a huge, boiling stew in the kitchen and wore his apron like a prized coat. When the neighborhood folks began to appear, he helped greet them and seat them. He hand-fed hot soup to one grateful gentleman who was missing fingers from both hands. He wiped off tables after each sitting and eagerly dispensed fresh plates to wave after wave of the hungry and homeless who came into the church hall. The other twenty or so youngsters, working with members of the church youth group, noticed the animated young man with the soft hands who seemed truly inspired by this opportunity to know and do real goodness in behalf of others.

Ryan continues to serve humanity in ways that were unknown to him before his first visit to the church kitchen. He smiles much more than he used to, and wrote a prize-winning essay about urban hunger in one of our community newspapers. He has organized a number of clothing drives and tells me that he may want to pursue a career in urban planning. He has more friends than ever before, and tells me that he often admonishes his father that giving money to the hunger fund is very fine but that actually giving a warm plate of food to a living human being is even finer.

"I know that my family will still help me to make it some day when I grow up," he recently told me. "But I really feel successful right now."

I worry about families in which hard-boiled notions of success define what parents and children are talking about. In the breadth of my congregation, I see a number of Ryans—youngsters from very wealthy families who suffer from a poverty of spirit, and others from modest families who love life and who enjoy themselves thoroughly. "Success" is a personal thing; it can't be quantified on a financial chart! We have to instill a strong sense of identity in every child we meet, regardless of their economic circumstances. In a 1992 report called *The Middle School—and Beyond*, Paul S. George and his coauthors stated: "Students appreciate and value teachers who help them become successful in ways that establish their individual worth and respectability in the eyes of peers and their parents." Young people may carry wallets but what they possess are souls.

Success, in any category, does not guarantee happiness or health. I have seen it so often: A financially independent person contracts an illness, recruits the finest medical care in the most exotic places, but still succumbs to the inevitable. Shrouds have no pockets. We are all made of flesh and blood, no matter how many dollars we may control or how often we can get the best table in a restaurant or the fastest booking with a hairdresser. We ought to demand of our children that they be creative and that they have healthy ambitions. But when we define success by applying external standards instead of internal feelings, then we really risk alienating a young person from himself exactly at the time in life when that youngster is formulating a set of values.

I went to see my friend Dave recently. Dave, the father of four magnificent children, inherited a service station from his wife's father many years ago. Dave works hard repairing automobiles and dealing with customers. He loves to read, he appreciates good music, and would have likely been an accomplished architect. Dave is a brilliant and sensitive individual who might have been doing other things under different circumstances. But he wouldn't trade his life for anything; his home is filled with laughter and tenderness. "I really have it all," he told me. He put on a fresh shirt and scrubbed the automobile grime from his fingers. He was clean, relaxed, and eager for the two of us to go out, along with our wives. There are few people that Cathy and I cherish as much as this wonderful couple who are unimaginably rich.

How do you know when you are successful in life? When you stop asking yourself this question and instead find ways to enrich your soul at least as much as you attempt to enrich your pocketbook.

CHAPTER 21

Why Do My Parents
Not Understand Some Things
That Are Obvious to Me?

S ari, my elder daughter, must have been asking herself the above question when her mother and I "lost it" about the clothes from the thrift shop. What we lost was our tempers; what we gained was a difficult and painful couple of days of confrontation with our child.

Don't ask me exactly why Sari and, evidently, some of her friends were on a thrift shop kick. It had become fashionable to acquire previously worn raiments at one of these worthy establishments that permit people of lesser means to purchase used clothing at low prices. The fact is that Sari is fortunate enough to be able to get clothing at traditional stores and that most of her friends are similarly blessed. Cathy and I found the new preoccupation peculiar, unnecessary and, I have to admit, somewhat embarrassing. We realized that this latter emotion was ultimately superficial, but were nonetheless unable to shake the nagging sense that Sari's wearing of these plaids and zigzags suggested that we had failed to be proper providers. Parents will do that to themselves, it would seem.

We eventually talked this out with Sari, but not before an extended exchange of anger and recriminations. I wound up dropping off my distraught daughter at the home of her dearest soulmate because Sari found herself "unable to stay in this house tonight." Watching her enter her friend's house, I saw the two embrace through the doorway. They shared some knowledge, some kindred spirit that definitely denied their parents' well of insights, and in which they gave one another a kind of comforting defiance. I certainly felt what all parents sometimes know—absolute exclusion from whatever is going on in the minds of their children. I thought the whole thing was all about a handful of garments. It was actually much more: Neither her mother nor I could possibly understand what was so obvious to our daughter—her need to express something about herself in the form of these thrift shop transactions.

Was it an oblique identification with the poor people who had sold their clothing for other needy folks to buy? In the 1960s, we had donned headbands, bleached shirts, and torn jeans in order to properly identify with the pain of one set of masses or the other. We protested our own relative affluence by looking tattered and socially conscious. I remember that the kids who came from the most comfortable homes usually looked the most like wandering hippies. These were also the youngsters who, like me, were least likely to ever serve in Vietnam or actually volunteer, hands-on, for the War on Poverty. Our parents didn't understand us; our heavy moral burden was as plain to us as the oversized rainbow sticker plastered across the back of our friend's redeeming and socially correct Volkswagen Beetle.

Meanwhile, what Cathy and I eventually made known to Sari was our opinion that the thrift shop adventure was ultimately misplaced. If you're going to purchase such clothing, why not donate it to any of the myriad of good causes that help people become clothed and fed? We accepted that Sari wanted to do something with the money she had herself earned at a part-time job, but wanted her to accept the implications of responsibility that came with her combination of sympathy for the underprivileged and the need to express herself. Sari asserted that she wanted the thrift shop clothing because it was socially stylish among her friends to have such garments, and that she felt that she had the right to be her creative self.

As with most things, we eventually came to a partial understanding of positions and a further realization that people from separate generations have separate perspectives. There are some ideals, some personal matters, even some secrets that Sari must keep from us. If we parents "got" everything, there would be no room for our children to grow on their own. The thrift shop episode in our home sharpened the lines of communication without violating any of the very precious and private realms of awareness that a youngster must have.

The fact is that young people have differing views of the world—both in comparison to adults and to each other. I recall a mother who told me a fascinating story about her twin girls, who were both fourteen years old when the Persian Gulf war broke out in 1991. In spite of their biological similitude, one is more sensitive than the other. They do not understand things in exactly the same way. It turns out that, as in so many households, the televised accounts of the swift but bitter conflict between Iraq and the U.S.-led coalition penetrated and affected the mind-sets of both parents and children. For some, the Scud missile attacks on Israeli cities and towns were particularly upsetting. For teenagers, this was the first American war they directly observed and noted.

It was fairly late at night when one of the twin girls entered her parents' bedroom, apparently anxious and worked up. She approached her mother at the bedside: "Mom," she murmured, in between sniffles. "Tell me something. When . . . when will the war end?"

The mother, obviously remembering her own childhood during the Vietnam era, stroked her daughter's hair. "It won't last so long," she reassured her child. "The one I went through at your age actually lasted for thirteen years. Things are different now. This will probably only take a couple of weeks. I understand how you feel."

Not more than a half-hour later, the other twin appeared by her mother's side. The mother anticipated a similar outbreak of nerves and concern. She took her other daughter's hand immediately. "What?" she asked.

"Mom," said this one, with some uneasiness. The mother prepared herself. "When . . . when can I get my own phone?"

You can never be sure what youngsters care about, or what moves them into action. I found myself turning to a group of teenagers one night about a subject that I was certain motivates them—the balance between humans and the natural environment. It was during a community discussion group; we had had good and meaningful deliberations on a variety of topics ranging from the separation of church and state to the need for drug-related laws to the changing geography of the post-Soviet world. Although interest in these topics varied, the kids' participation belied the charge of cranial inertia often directed against today's teenagers. Once or twice, they raised issues that were obviously important to them, such as what kind of music that kids in England preferred or the impropriety of polyester slacks. My receptivity to these matters was negligible, although I had to concede that my lack of comprehension was only as complete as their absorption in these and certain other generation-related concerns. I suppose, therefore, that I could have forgiven the youngsters' indifference one night to my introduction of the question of Idaho woodpeckers.

It had become evident during a recent autumn that pileated woodpeckers in the vicinity of the Salmon River were drilling holes in power poles that service communities in the Idaho mountain ranges. The black-and-white and crimson birds have a need to peck wooden posts for the purpose of making nests or finding insects. The drilling into the man-made poles was leaving some of these towers vulnerable to the coming winter weather. Fallen power lines were an obvious hardship for the somewhat isolated mountain towns.

"Here is a case where God's natural order and the needs of modern humans are coming into conflict," I told the youngsters, earnestly. "These woodpeckers are feasting on the power lines because there has been a drought in the area. When trees are weakened by a lack of water, more insects invade them. Now the woodpeckers have been flocking into the area to feed on the insects, but the wood-peckers don't particularly care if they're pecking on a tree or a local power-company line. Isn't that something?"

Well, my students were as indifferent to this predica-ment as the woodpeckers were to what kind of wood they were hammering. It seemed like such an obvious crisis to me, an exemplary case of the environmental dilemma. I went home that evening, fairly certain that none of my Ohio youngsters was going to dread an Idaho woodpecker when he or she flipped the power switch on the CD player.

Indeed, we speak different languages, kids and adults. This applies even to the subject of the compact disc player. It was not so long ago when I attempted to explain my nostalgic concern for the fate of record albums to Sari—a subject of deep solicitude for me but only polite attentive-ness for my Discman-toting teenaged child.

I had taken Sari down into our family den, where, in the dusty shadows adjacent to the coaxial lines that connect our television set to thirty-nine cable possibilities, there lies a beaten, old wicker box. At my behest, Sari opened the box and exclaimed: "Cool! Old magazines! The covers are harder than regular magazines."

"No, love," I said, my throat tightening a bit with wist-fulness. "These are not magazines. These are record al-bums." Sari realized this immediately, but I was determined to fulfill my postmodern anxiety. "These used to be sold in places called record stores. They were played on things called record players. I guess that was before your time," I finished, my soul a turntable of self-pity.

"My friends and I go to the Record Exchange," my daughter replied with encouragement. "But that's where we buy tapes and CDs. So, these are records?"

"I guess they're more like mementos," I answered.

In comparing notes with Sari about record albums and compact discs, I soon realized that it was simply a matter of two different eras. Why should she understand my nostalgia for a long-playing, vinyl record? That's what people played during my adolescence; the CD is what youngsters use now. Sari would not be able to actually comprehend my angst on this any more than I actually understood my parents' nostalgia or righteousness on a myriad of notions and devices from their time. The chances are that Sari will one day fail to fathom the technological musical mechanism that her son or daughter will be showing her. It all has to do with the inevitable seasons of human life.

I conceded to Sari that compact discs and digital tape recordings make flawless sound. But seeking the perfect world, we act like life never has static. No, there are some things that one generation cannot understand about the other. The vinyl record, with double-breasted jacket and full-sized photos, turning at a regal 33⅓ speed, was weighty, vulnerable, and it invoked responsibility. There are more serious issues between parents and children, but the memory of my silent record albums, and Sari's understandable preference for her efficient, mobile shiny discs serve to remind me of a long-playing reality—the generation gap.

The fact is we live in different worlds, our children and us. We both need a repository for our memories and our sensibilities—be it a wicker box or a CD filing stack. What's important is that, from time to time, we allow one another a glimpse of the storage cases, if not a full disclosure of the contents. Meanwhile, why do parents not understand some things that would seem so obvious to children? Because parents and children think about and value different things, from thrift shops to woodpeckers to record albums to the meaning of life.

CHAPTER 22

Why Is the World
Always in My Face?

The above question was heard in the year 1968, just outside Woodward High School in Cincinnati, Ohio. It was spoken to whomever was within earshot by my indomitable friend and cohort, Clifton Fleetwood. Clifton—black, brash, infinitely skinny, and remarkably musical—was the drum major in our Woodward High School marching band. He was also an incorrigible complainer who had the ability to get himself into serious trouble with any teacher at just about any given moment. We were both in tenth grade that year, both marching in the band—when the Vietnam War was consuming hundreds of American youngsters weekly, when the political process seemed as shaky as the streets outside the Chicago Democratic National Convention, and included the racist intonations of presidential candidate George Wallace, when gunfire destroyed both Martin Luther King, Jr. and Senator Robert F. Kennedy within weeks of each other, when American cities burned in anger from the spring through the summer.

Clifton was as jocular as he was wiry. He preferred mirth to the gathering gloom of our high school experiences; the national mood reverberated through the hallways of our integrated, increasingly tense school building. One day, a week or so after Dr. King was murdered, and black activists were trying to convince Clifton and others like him to boycott classes, my friend blurted out, in frustration and discouragement: "Why is the world always in my face?"

Like any other sixteen year old in 1968 or in 1995, Clifton wanted the noise to abate, the pressure to ease, the fear to evaporate. But it would not be so, because, as the rabbinic tradition intoned centuries ago: "The world is too much with us."

I know a kid today, Zachary, who often wonders why the outside world seems to invade his private life so much. "You can't get away from it," he sighs, before returning his stereophonic personal headphones back into place. Zachary is not listening to chamber music, however. He "escapes" from what's in the newspaper into an inner audio chamber of lyrics, chords, strumming, and modulation that no doubt resounds with the prevailing themes of today: violence, sex, drug abuse, and intrigue. My point is not necessarily to decry what is heard through the earphones, but to suggest that contemporary music—like the talk shows and a significant segment of motion pictures—is but another expression of the current cultural intrusiveness.

You can't get away from, nor deny too much of it. In

the opening of his novel, *The Ice Storm*, Rick Moody offers a fantasy:

No answering machines. And no call waiting. No Caller I.D. No compact disc recorders or laser discs or holography or cable television or MTV. No multiplex cinemas or word processors or laser printers or modems. No virtual reality. No computer viruses. No cloning or genetic engineering or biospheres or full-color photocopying or desktop copying and especially no facsimile transmission.

It's perhaps understandable that a youngster will grow weary of all the information, ideological implementation, and frequency modulation that indent the paragraphs of his or her being. Young people, like adults, depend upon the codes, the credit card strips, and the coaxial lines as sure as we sometimes grumble about them. It's human nature to mutter about our living environment now, just as surely as our ancestors cursed their leaky oil stoves, their smoky Model T automobiles, and their intermittent plumbing. But rest assured that they desired to cook, to travel, and to wash their faces.

Granted, today's teenagers are bombarded by the cybernetic and electrical and videogenic components that inextricably link everyone across a rushing, information superhighway. A tonnage of data and a certain din pervade our households, all entering from without the walls of the house, through miles and miles of wiring and optic fibers. It remains for every parent to help his or her child find some balance in the process of modern living. Every day, we should look, listen, and love. But when a child complains about the world being "in his face," we need to help that child form a perspective. No matter what, it is good to be alive enough to acknowledge the world, even if the world occasionally requires an adjustment of the volume knob.

There once was a fifteen year old whom I shall never forget—although I never met the boy. His sudden death on a Cleveland basketball court has permanently affected me. Drew was the same age in 1994 that I was in that watershed year of 1968, when I was just beginning to truly decipher the sometimes incongruous, voluminous invasion of the world's business into my private consciousness. Drew was apparently good-natured and certainly athletic. His adolescent body evidently held a secret that spilled onto the gymnasium floor of a local community center during an international tournament that our town was hosting. The young man's heart had simply stopped. I was one of several rabbis and other professionals called upon to be with Drew's Louisville teammates and Boston opponents in the hours after his demise.

It fell to me and to a thoughtful man named Adolfo, the leader of the Louisville delegation, to actually tell the boys and girls that Drew had died. The players—Louisville in blue and Boston in red—were taken to a conference room in the building where they awaited some word.

It was not known to these innocent youngsters that Drew's short life ended after his collapse. All they saw was the emergency scene, and Drew being whisked away on a stretcher. We grown-ups were now presented with a situation much larger than ourselves. Some 2,500 young athletes had gathered in Cleveland to fulfill the human spirit.

What do we do? What do we say? How do we control the situation?

Rabbis, social workers, and administrators crowded together into an office across the hall from the forlorn and waiting ballplayers. Some of the Louisville parents filled the hallways (Drew's family was not present); they were anxious, impatient, scared. They basically knew what happened and held on to the knowledge that their own children were safe. But everyone understood that in that conference room, still dressed in sports regalia, were thirty young people who in a few moments would no longer be children.

How do you tell teenagers that life is sometimes dreadfully limited? How do you, for example, explain sudden and inexplicable death? What is your point when dealing with strong and competitive youngsters who regard nothing as impossible, who are connected to so many power sources, and who think of life itself as an unobstructed running path? Now, thought Adolfo and I, literally holding onto each other, how do we tell these kids that Drew was dead?

Adolfo and I entered the silent room. The youngsters sat around the conference table like so many prisoners of terrible circumstances. I was grateful that Adolfo was there; he and I were strangers to each other who became intimately and forever linked through this tragedy. But the kids from Louisville knew him and his face; we were counting upon that familiarity to take us through the next few moments.

Adolfo stared at them for a few seconds. They read his eyes, his tightening cheeks, his nervous hands. He was unable to say anything immediately. I spoke up, a kind of reluctant guest host who would have given anything to be anywhere else but in that room.

"Friends, your director has something to tell you. I am a rabbi and my temple is next door. After he speaks to you, I will answer questions you have, and we will both listen carefully to what you may want to say."

The Louisville players appeared more edgy now. The Boston teammates, who had been guilty of only wanting to win a ball game, withdrew even more into their corner of remorse. I made a mental note to tell Boston that it wasn't their fault.

Adolfo spoke, his voice trapped somewhere between his heart and his throat. "The news is not good. . . . Drew passed away. . . . I'm sorry to tell you. . . ." Heads bobbed, hands were thrown up, sobs burst, eyes shut, bodies fell together in anguished support. Adolfo and I held arms. Unbelievably, we had not known each other when we awoke that morning.

We then left the young people pretty much to themselves. It seemed they needed time to absorb the shock. A few other sympathetic adults came in and out of the conference room. None of us were absolutely sure of what we were doing.

It became apparent that these kids had to get out of that room. It was closing in on them. But how to take them out into the crowded community-center building, filled with athletes and events, without causing a greater panic and hysteria? Drew's family had been informed in Louisville. Our responsibility was to the sports village that had been created and was now threatened.

My synagogue was next door. We decided to retreat there and allow these youngsters space and support. In a few moments, a handful of us adults led the blue-and-red group out a back door. We walked across a gravel road and a grassy hill to the synagogue. Each of us surely felt like Moses leading an exodus of wounded children.

An extended and informal staff of counselors, clergymen, and caring parents joined us for the next several hours. The synagogue staff turned over their desks, their chairs, their telephones to needful children who wanted to call their parents back home. Meals were brought over. Large and small groups interrelated, cried, emoted and, tentatively, began to heal.

At one point, a delegation of three Boston players came over to the room where the Louisville team sat together. "We are sorry about what happened to Drew," said their spokesman. "We want your permission to go and play our afternoon game against Mexico, and to wear Drew's number on our uniform." Hearing the words of this remarkable teenager who stood there in his warm-up suit, his arms hanging awkwardly and eyes watering up, we adults just stared at each other. We suddenly knew what to do: We just needed to keep on listening to these young people. And we also knew that we must hold our own children more closely than ever.

Granted, the account of a young athlete suddenly dying on a basketball court represents a rare instance. But the reality of trouble, whether in this form, or through the many and unending manifestations of death, danger, and social dysfunction that teenagers encounter through the media, and in their own real lives, add up to my friend

Clifton's old complaint: "Why is the world always in my face?"

For today's teenagers, there is a great deal that is "in their faces." They are affected and informed by all of it. Most affecting for them, however, is what they know at home. What is mostly "in their faces" is the physical and spiritual reflection of the parents who gave them life in the first place. So when a youngster, in one form or another, asks why the world is in his or her face, the answer is because you and I are lucky enough to be alive together.

AFTERWORD

❧

From Drugs to Dating
to Destiny: What Do We Say
to Our Teenagers?

Above all, we should not be disingenuous with our children. Even when it's well-intended, such an approach will not work. As I've said throughout this book, teenagers know too much, feel too much, and need too much in order to be fooled by even a benevolent craftiness. In a number of areas, they have more experience than we think they do.

The issue of drugs comes to mind. As suggested here, teenagers have a high level of awareness about drugs. A frightening proportion of teenagers—many from affluent homes—have experimented with them or are using them. My own daughters tell me that the sight of drug abuse is not uncommon in their school buildings; I understand (and continue to hope they won't waver) that my daughters' decisions to abstain are not necessarily typical. I also feel for my daughters when they make such decisions (regarding drugs, as well as alcohol and sex), because they are making these positive choices against the grain of significant peer pressure.

I tell my daughters that I am proud of them for their instincts on such things as drugs, and I also vocalize my admiration for them on the matter of the social pressure. I believe that they need this reinforcement, even as I hope that my praise is still more important to them than the approbation of some of their classmates who have lost their way.

I also make it clear: Drugs are not negotiable. There is no middle ground, no room for concessions. We have often agreed in our house that drugs are pretty much the same things as guns. Drugs are killers. You should talk about this openly with your kids. Let them share all the details about drugs that they already know. Their knowledge of these substances (much of it garnered in their school classroom) may shock you a bit. You may not have thought they had such an awareness. What you should do is congratulate them for it, and exalt them when it is clear that they know enough about drugs to condemn them in every category.

The more directly you are involved in the discussion of drugs and alcohol with your teenage children, the more you will be manifest in their minds when they make the decision to use or not use drugs. Don't distance yourself from this or any other topic; you will only increase the distance between you and your child.

This principle of thoughtful involvement with your teenager is the number-one message of this book. Don't stand on ceremony with your kid; if he or she isn't receptive to a discussion, just back off for a little while. Don't get angry because your pride was wounded, or because you have some notion that your teenager was rude or impertinent. Crises involving drugs, alcohol, or pregnancy don't ameliorate because of a better social atmosphere. These issues burst into teenagers' lives, and either we are facilitators for their lives or we are simply caretakers. To paraphrase an old adage, a parent should be part of the solution, not part of the problem.

Let's face it: We aren't as fast as MTV, as slick as *YM* magazine, or as spellbinding as Pearl Jam. But we are still the parents—flesh-and-blood connections between these kids and creation. Even while being distracted by the imperial characters of *Beverly Hills 90210*, they will still admit in their emerging hearts that they need us and that they crave our love.

Ask yourself: What are you doing, every day, for the welfare and security of your teenage child? Yes, you go to work, earn a living, and provide material comforts. But on a deeper level, what do you know about that person in the next room? Are you aware of her dreams? Do you know what ails him? Do you know who he or she loves or hates? Do you know, categorically, if he or she uses drugs? Granted, no parent can absolutely know everything (and kids are entitled to privacy in some instances), but you should have an *inkling* of what's going on in the life of your teenager.

One of the most difficult things for parents to embrace is their child's growth and development. We actually resent their emerging involvement in dating, socializing, and all the associated ramifications. It's hard for us to accept that "our baby" is suddenly being picked up in an automobile by some other teenager, motoring off to some party, rendezvousing with a group whom we suspect of every felonious activity under the sun, or attending a late-night movie that we are sure they're all too young to see. It's hard for us to let go of our teenagers' evaporated innocence. We get angry and suspicious of them for being something that we don't want them to be. Meanwhile, all they want to be is themselves.

A good guideline for most any household dealing with the reality of new relationships: Calm down. Be reasonable, while gently demanding information. You have a right to know where your teenager is at any time. You have the right and responsibility to establish reasonable time restrictions. Your teenager also has the natural right to explore his or her growth, to make friends, to experience romantic feelings, and to keep some things to himself or herself. The answer to how we handle our teenagers in this and every category (except drugs) is always somewhere in between. Find a middle ground between scrutiny and watchfulness. Your child *wants* you to care about his or her situations, even if he or she doesn't want you to be privy to everything.

Being a parent is hard work. It is not always rewarded with gratitude or even with a smile. Both parents and children sometimes fail in the category of rectitude. People are imperfect beings; adolescence is probably the most imperfect and awkward passages in life. Beyond all this, we are not living in an era that is especially kind to children.

I remember visiting a suburban high school not too long ago to speak about the problems of American minorities.

The school in question is in a predominately white, blue-collar section; there are not too many Jews or African-Americans in the student body. Nevertheless, about seventy juniors were taking an elective class on this subject that meets at 7:20 in the morning!

Albeit it was early, I did not find this group of teenagers to be altogether receptive or motivated. They had meager knowledge of some basic things I raised with them, such as the population figures of the United States, the dates of the Second World War, or the geography of their own state and region. When I asked them about their heroes, I received mostly sarcastic answers, such as "O. J. Simpson, right?" or "nobody in Congress." Their vocabulary was average at best, even though they were hardly a stupid bunch of youngsters.

I understood that half of them come from broken homes, and noticed that few of them looked me in the eye. I felt for these teenagers. Their teachers were earnest, sincere, and caring. With a few exceptions, I sensed that most of these fairly typical American high school students were going through the motions of coming to class and basically dispensing with the process. They are not excited or even angry about much of anything.

It all gave me an uncomfortable feeling. Something is missing in our society. After the session, I ventured into the hallways of this fairly standard public school. The paint on the walls was peeling. The windows were not so clean. Looking outside, I noticed that there was garbage strewn along the walkways. In the washroom, there were no mirrors. That created the sensation of emptiness for me, a certain lack of human presence. "The community never passes the school levies," one teacher told me, accounting for the tawdriness of the institution.

As a society, we don't care enough for our children! In many places, they are hungry; in many places, they are also spiritually malnourished. This is not a political book, but the lack of healthy priorities in our civilization speaks for itself. Meanwhile, when I encounter a group of indifferent and uninspired teenagers sitting through a meaningful course early in the morning in a school with no mirrors, I wonder what the view really is that reflects back on our children.

Into this situation are thrust the parents of a generation that faces a new century with plenty of manufactured information but not enough heartfelt enthusiasm. They are unsure of their destiny and skeptical of the future. They certainly are not well-trained in the meaning of the past. Their best hopes are their families. Their finest protectors are their parents.

We are the ones who created them. We are the ones collectively responsible for the world they inherit. Before it's too late, we ought to give them completely of ourselves—from attention to discipline to forgiveness. The one thing that should never be denied any young person is the certainty that at home someone is looking, listening, and loving.

The typeface used in this book is a version of Caledonia, originally designed by William A. Dwiggins (1880–1956), who also designed Electra. Starting as a graphic artist and book designer (he called himself a "black and white-smith"), he came late to type design, even though he was from his youth an associate of Frederick Goudy, the preeminent American type designer of the time. Caledonia was designed on a challenge from Mergenthaler Linotype: to keep the successful aspects of the popular if not very attractive font, Scotch Roman (so called because it was first cut in Scotland)—its large lowercase letters with generous "counters" (internal spaces)—and to rid it of flaws, especially its overly dark capitals. Dwiggins' strategy was to blend it with elements of another "modern," Bulmer, and in the end he created one of the most attractive typefaces in use today.